LifeLight™
FOUNDATIONS

"In Him was life, and the life was the light of men." John 1:4

Time between the Testaments

LEADERS GUIDE

CONCORDIA PUBLISHING HOUSE • SAINT LOUIS

Tobias and his dog walk among angels as they return to Nineveh, where his parents, Tobit and Anna, count the days, awaiting his return. The story of this Naphtalite family tells us much about the beliefs and practices of God's people during the Time between the Testaments—both good and bad. In *Tobias and the Three Archangels*, Florentine artist Francesco di Giovanni Botticini (1446–98) illustrates the people's faith that the Lord and His angels were watching over them. As you read the stories of these Israelites, step into their shoes. Feel the pressure of persecution they experienced as well as the presence of the Lord's angels.

3558 S. Jefferson Ave., St. Louis, MO 63118-3968
1-800-325-3040 • www.cph.org

Written by Lane A. Burgland

Edited by Edward A. Engelbrecht

COVER: The three archangels with Tobias, by Francesco Botticini. Art Archive,The/Art Archive,The

This publication may be available in Braille, in large print, or on cassette tape for the visually impaired. Please allow 8 to 12 weeks for delivery. Write to Lutheran Braille Workers, P.O. Box 5000, Yucaipa, CA 92399; call toll-free 1-800-925-6092; or visit the website: www.LBWinc.org.

Manufactured in the United States of America

1 2 3 4 5 6 7 8 9 10 24 23 22 21 20 19 18 17 16 15

Contents

Introduction

Welcome to LifeLight

A special pleasure is in store for you. You will be instrumental in leading your brothers and sisters in Christ closer to Him who is our life and light (John 1:4). You will have the pleasure of seeing fellow Christians discover new insights and rediscover old ones as they open the Scriptures and dig deep into them, perhaps deeper than they have ever dug before. More than that, you will have the pleasure of sharing in this wonderful study.

LifeLight—An In-depth Study

LifeLight is a series of in-depth Bible studies. The goal of LifeLight is that through a regular program of in-depth personal and group study of Scripture, more and more Christian adults may grow in their personal faith in Jesus Christ, enjoy fellowship with the members of His Body, and reach out in love to others in witness and service.

In-depth means that this Bible study includes the following four components: individual daily home study; discussion in a small group; a lecture presentation on the Scripture portion under study; and an enhancement of the week's material (through reading the enrichment magazine).

LifeLight Participants

LifeLight participants are adults who desire a deeper study of the Scriptures than is available in the typical Sunday morning adult Bible class. (Mid-to-older teens might also be LifeLight participants.) While LifeLight does not assume an existing knowledge of the Bible or special experience or skills in Bible study, it does assume a level of commitment that will bring participants to each of the nine weekly assemblies having read the assigned readings and attempted to answer the study questions. Daily reading and study will require from 15 to 30 minutes for the five days preceding the LifeLight assembly. The day following the assembly will be spent reviewing the previous week's study by going over the completed study leaflet and the enrichment magazine.

LifeLight Leadership

While the in-depth process used by LifeLight begins with individual study and cannot achieve its aims without this individual effort, it cannot be completed by individual study alone. Therefore, trained leaders are necessary. You fill one or perhaps more of the important roles described below.

The Director

This person oversees the LifeLight program in a local center (which may be a congregation or a center operated by several neighboring congregations). The director

- serves as the parish LifeLight overall coordinator and leader;
- coordinates the scheduling of the LifeLight program;
- orders materials;
- convenes LifeLight leadership-team meetings;
- develops publicity materials;
- recruits participants;
- maintains records and budgeting;
- assigns, with the leadership team, participants to small discussion groups;
- makes arrangements for facilities;
- communicates outreach opportunities to small-group leaders and to congregational boards;
- follows up on participants who leave the program.

The Assistant Director *(optional)*

This person may assist the director. Duties listed for the director may be assigned to the assistant director as mutually agreeable.

The Lecture Leader

This person prepares and delivers the lecture at the weekly assembly. ***(Lesson material for the lecture leader begins on p. 8.)*** The lecture leader

- prepares and presents the Bible study lecture to the large group;

- prepares worship activities (devotional thought, hymn, prayer) using resources in the study leaflet and leaders guide and possibly other outside sources;
- helps the small-group discussion leaders to grow in understanding the content of the lessons;
- encourages prayer at weekly leadership-team and discussion leaders meetings.

The Small-Group Coordinator *(optional; the director may fill this role)*

This person supervises and coordinates the work of the small-group discussion leaders. The small-group coordinator

- recruits with the leadership-team the small-group discussion leaders;
- trains or arranges for training of the discussion leaders;
- assists the director and discussion leaders in follow-up and outreach;
- encourages the discussion leaders to contact absent group members;
- participates in the weekly leadership-team and discussion-leaders equipping meetings;
- provides ongoing training and support as needed.

The Small-Group Discussion Leaders

These people guide and facilitate discussion of LifeLight participants in the small groups. ***(Lesson material for the small-group leaders begins on p. 55.)*** There should be one discussion leader for every group of no more than twelve participants. The small-group discussion leaders are, perhaps, those individuals who are most important to the success of the program. They should, therefore, be chosen with special care and be equipped with skills needed to guide discussion and to foster a caring fellowship within the group. These discussion leaders

- prepare each week for the small-group discussion by using the study leaflet and small-group leaders guide section for that session *(see p. 55)*;
- read the enrichment magazine as a study supplement;
- guide and facilitate discussion in their small group;
- encourage and assist the discussion group in prayer;
- foster fellowship and mutual care within the discussion group;
- attend weekly discussion leaders training meetings.

Leadership Training

LifeLight leaders will meet weekly to review the previous week's work and plan the coming week. At this session, leaders can address concerns and prepare for the coming session. LifeLight is a 1½-hour program with no possibility for it to be taught in the one hour typically available on Sunday mornings. Some congregations, however, may want to use the Sunday-morning Bible study hour for LifeLight preparation and leadership training. In such a meeting, the lecture leader and/or small-group coordinator may lead the discussion leaders through the coming week's lesson, reserving five or ten minutes for problem solving or other group concerns.

While it requires intense effort, LifeLight has proven to bring great benefit to LifeLight participants. The effort put into this program, both by leaders and by participants, will be rewarding and profitable.

The LifeLight Weekly Schedule

Here is how LifeLight will work week by week:

1. Before session 1, each participant will receive the study leaflet for session 1 and the enrichment magazine for the course. The study leaflet contains worship resources (for use both in individual daily study and at the opening of the following week's assembly) and readings and study questions for five days. Challenge questions will lead those participants who have the time and desire a greater challenge into even deeper levels of study.

2. After the five days of individual study at home, participants will gather for a weekly assembly of all LifeLight participants. The assembly will begin with a brief period of worship (5 minutes). Participants will then join their assigned small discussion groups (of twelve or fewer, who will remain the same throughout the course), where they will go over the week's study questions together (55 minutes). Assembling together once again, participants will listen to a lecture presentation on the readings they have studied in the previous week and discussed in their small groups (20 minutes). After the lecture presentation, the director or another leader will distribute the study leaflet for the following week.

Closing announcements and other necessary business may take another five minutes before dismissal.

In some places, some small groups will not join the weekly assembly because of scheduling or other reasons. Such groups may meet at another time and place (perhaps in the home of one of the small group's members). Those congregations may record the lecture given by the lecture leader at the weekly assembly and duplicate it for use by other groups meeting later in the week.

3. On the day following the assembly, participants will review the preceding week's work by rereading the study leaflet they completed (and that they perhaps supplemented or corrected during the discussion in their small group) and by reading appropriate articles in the enrichment magazine.

Then the LifeLight weekly study process will begin all over again!

Recommended Study Resources and Worship

The Lutheran Study Bible. St. Louis: Concordia Publishing House, 2009. This resource contains more than 26,000 study and application notes, a most thorough reference guide (pp. lxv–cx), and more than 90,000 cross-references, as well as a 31,000-entry concordance, maps, charts, and timelines.

The Apocrypha: The Lutheran Edition with Notes. St. Louis: Concordia Publishing House, 2012. This study-Bible treatment of the Apocrypha includes an extensive introduction to the 400-year Time between the Testaments as well as maps, charts, illustrations, and extensive articles.

Roehrs, Walter R., and Martin H. Franzmann. *Concordia Self-Study Commentary.* St. Louis: Concordia Publishing House, 1979. This one-volume commentary on the Bible contains 950 pages and is tailored for lay use.

The Concordia Organist is a 31-CD collection of pipe organ accompaniments for all the hymns and liturgical music in *Lutheran Service Book*. St. Louis: Concordia Publishing House (order no. 99-2264). Use these CDs for worship hymn accompaniment.

Righteousness and Shame

Baruch; Letter of Jeremiah; Susanna

Preparing for the Session

Central Focus

In God's righteousness, He deals with sin by disciplining His people. The child of God responds by confessing all sin and turning to the wisdom of God for direction. Forgiven, God's people rejoice in their restoration accomplished in Christ Jesus.

Objectives

That participants, led by the Holy Spirit working through God's Word, will

1. seek the Lord in humility, confessing all sins and rejoicing in the full forgiveness won for them by Jesus Christ;

2. pray for others, especially leaders and the nation, that they might turn to the Lord and walk the path of wisdom; and

3. turn to the Lord in prayer and trust His Word when faced with trial or temptation.

Note for the small-group leaders: Lesson notes and other materials you will need begin on page 55.

For the Lecture Leader

Session Plan

Worship

Begin the session with the hymn printed in the study leaflet. Accompaniments are available in denominational hymnals, such as *Lutheran Service Book* or *Lutheran Worship* (refer to hymnal index). (Note: Concordia Publishing House has available *The Concordia Organist*. All the initial worship hymns in the LifeLight courses are included in this resource. It's especially helpful for mission congregations and small parishes. See the list of study resources on p. 7.) Follow with this prayer:

Prayer

Father, forgive us for our sins, washing us thoroughly in the blood of Your Son, our Savior, Jesus Christ. Lead us today and always by Your Holy Spirit to live wisely, according to Your Word. Keep us faithful in all trial and temptation, wiping away the deception of the world and the darkness of sin. Lift up our eyes from the present troubles to the day when You call us home, filling us with the sure and certain hope of our resurrection to eternal life through our Lord, Jesus Christ. Amen.

Lecture Presentation

Introduction

"Not again!"

As the people of God felt the sting of defeat at the hand of a Gentile enemy and saw the desecration of their temple once more, they might have cried out, "Not again!" Jerusalem had fallen several centuries earlier to the Babylonians, who had destroyed the temple and carried off their ancestors to Babylon, hundreds of miles away. Jeremiah had eloquently expressed the peoples' grief in the Book of Lamentations. They learned their lesson. The faithful remnant returned from Babylon at the end of the sixth century BC and, with a little encouragement from Ezra and Nehemiah, remained faithful to God. Or so they thought.

The mid-fifth century BC marks the beginning of a "silent time" when no prophet from God appears to speak to His people. Yet, four long centuries later, the greatest prophet of all time would arise in the wilderness, preaching the kingdom of God and baptizing people for the forgiveness of sins (Luke 7:26–28). Between Malachi and John the Baptist, however, God seemed silent, even though His people faced terrible suffering and oppression.

In their day, a foreign enemy would once again devastate the city and defile the Holy Place, the temple of God. On the temple's altar, in 167 BC, Antiochus IV Epiphanes would sacrifice a pig—an animal unfit for sacrifice or human consumption among Israelites—to the pagan god Zeus. Antiochus would try to force the population to abandon their faith and adopt Greek religion and culture. He burned the Hebrew Scriptures and put their owners to death. He required people to eat "unclean" foods to demonstrate their compliance with the new laws and banned circumcision.

How had Israel come to this yet again?

1 Introduction *(Baruch 1:1–14)*

To explain the suffering during the Time between the Testaments, the author of Baruch looks back over four centuries to the time when Jerusalem fell to the forces of Babylonian king Nebuchadnezzar in 587 BC. The Babylonians had taken many of the best and brightest to Babylon in two earlier deportations (605 BC and 597 BC). Prophets like Daniel and Ezekiel (in Babylon) and Jeremiah (in Jerusalem) called people to repentance and renewed obedience, but their message fell on deaf ears. The city fell and sacrifices at the temple ceased.

The author of this first book takes on the persona of Baruch, secretary to Jeremiah. He may have intended his readers to understand that he wasn't the real Baruch, whom Jeremiah tells us was in Egypt (see Jeremiah 43:1–7). This thought is reinforced when the fictional Baruch takes some of the temple's vessels back to Jerusalem, where sacrifices would still be made. Baruch 1:10–18 even contains instructions to read the book in the "house of the Lord" (the temple) on a regular basis—hard to do, since the temple was destroyed in Jeremiah's day (see 2 Kings 25).

In his introduction, the author of Baruch asks his readers to put themselves in the sandals of their ancestors. We might hear him say to his contemporaries, "Remember! Remember when the Gentiles destroyed our city and defiled our temple. Remember the sin of our ancestors and the justice of God. Remember the mercy of God as He forgave His penitent people and eventually restored to them their city and its temple. Remember and repent, come to the Lord with a broken heart and a contrite spirit, and He will again forgive and restore." His instructions to read the book regularly (1:14) challenge his readers to humble themselves before the Lord in the hope that He would forgive them and once again lift them up (see also James 4:10; 1 Peter 5:6).

2 Confession and Prayer *(Baruch 1:15–3:8)*

Baruch repeats 1:15 at 2:6 to signal the approaching close of his confession before moving into a prayer for deliverance. Somewhat similar to Daniel's prayer several centuries earlier (see Daniel 9), the author portrays Baruch interceding for God's people. Baruch affirms that the blame for all that has happened falls squarely on the people—none of it is God's fault. By their disobedience, they have earned the curse of God as laid out in the Mosaic code (see Deuteronomy 28:15–68).

Baruch explains the sufferings of God's people as a just punishment from God against sin. The Word of God would challenge this overly simplistic explanation of human suffering, both in the Book of Job as well as in the New Testament. In John 9, for example, the disciples ask Jesus if a man who was born blind suffered because of his own sin or because of his parents' sin. Jesus answered that the man's sufferings were not due to any specific sin but so that the works of God could be displayed in him (through the healing that Jesus was about to accomplish; vv. 9:1–7). Similarly, Peter tells us that God uses sufferings to purify and strengthen faith (see 1 Peter 1:3–9). Ultimately, God punishes all sin by taking upon Himself the curse of the Law in the person of His Son, Jesus Christ, crucified and risen from the dead (see Romans 3:21–31; Galatians 3:13–14). He does, however, discipline His people (Hebrews 12:3–11).

In Baruch 2:27–3:8, the author "turns the corner" from a recounting of the past to addressing the present and appeals to God based on His promises and His name. Echoing Moses (Deuteronomy 30:1–6) and Ezekiel (Ezekiel 36:16–28), the fictional Baruch lays claim to God's promise of forgiveness and restoration. He asks the Lord to forget the past sins and save the people to demonstrate His power and faithfulness to the world (note especially Baruch 3:5). By saving and restoring His people, the name of God will be glorified (as Jesus Himself says in John 12:28–32; 13:31–32; 17:1–5). As the New Testament people of God, we realize that only in Christ Jesus do we know God and only in His cross do we find the forgiveness Baruch seeks.

3 A Poem of Wisdom *(Baruch 3:9–4:4)*

Baruch's poem on wisdom resembles the biblical teaching on wisdom but reflects his own specific definition in the end. For example, Job 28 records Job's quest for wisdom in the midst of his own suffering. He ultimately concludes (v. 28) "the fear of the Lord, that is wisdom, and to turn away from evil is understanding." The phrase "the fear of the Lord" in the Bible reflects a much broader picture than modern readers might suppose. It includes the sinner's fear of punishment by a righteous

God as well as the respect and awe the creature has for its Creator. More important, when described as a foundation for wisdom, it denotes saving faith in the one true God and a willingness to follow His directives (see also Psalm 130:4; Acts 9:31; 10:34–35).

The fictional Baruch offers a very clearly focused definition of wisdom as the written Word of God. Given only to Israel (Baruch 3:36), wisdom becomes Torah—the Hebrew Scriptures, especially the Books of Moses (Baruch 3:37–4:1a). Baruch would say that the path of wisdom is utter and complete devotion to keeping the Mosaic Law (4:1b).

The biblical view of wisdom would certainly include the Scriptures, but it sees the broader picture behind that. We might say that in the Bible, wisdom is relational—it flows from a personal relationship with the Lord through His Word. Paul certainly takes us in that direction, traveling to the cross to find true wisdom. Christ Jesus is Himself the power and wisdom of God (see 1 Corinthians 1:18–25).

4 Encouragement for Israel *(Baruch 4:5–5:9)*

Drawing on Isaiah 40–66 and other Scriptures, the author of Baruch reaches out to his contemporaries with a word of encouragement and hope. Just as the exile to Babylon had ended with a return of God's people to Jerusalem and a rebuilding of the temple in the past (sixth to fifth centuries BC), so the Lord would bring to an end the present calamities and would restore the temple and Jerusalem. God used the exile and sacrilege Antiochus IV Epiphanes committed in 167 BC and the subjection of His people to the Gentiles to call His people back to Him.

Baruch challenges the reader to trust God for deliverance, a very difficult thing to do in the midst of hardship. We tend to look at the circumstances and don't see beyond the troubles of the present. As a result, we do not see the larger picture, nor do we experience the comfort and peace of knowing God is working all things for good, for the salvation of people (see Romans 8:28). Matthew 16:21–23 offers an excellent example of this human tendency. Having confessed Jesus as the Christ, the Son of the living God, Peter then rejects Jesus' plan and goal—the cross. He does not understand the real problem of sin; nor does he appreciate the radical solution: God Incarnate, crucified for the sins of the world.

Can God's people trust Him to save them? Likely centuries before Christ would come, Baruch answers a resounding "Yes!"—assuming they will repent and return to Him with a fresh commitment to keep His Law.

5 The Letter of Jeremiah

The purpose of this letter is to expose the utter folly of worshiping idols instead of the true God. God's people have always had to deal with the temptation to worship something or someone else other than the true God. In the past, these false gods took the form of idols made of wood or stone or precious metals. In present Western culture, false gods may take other forms: money, fame, power, social acceptance, even life itself. We can benefit from the point made by the author of this letter, even though the form and shape of the idols have changed.

In verses 2–7, the author warns of a long captivity—up to seven generations. The prophet Jeremiah had predicted the exile would last seventy years (Jeremiah 25:11–12; 29:10) and a remnant, perhaps as many as 50,000 people, did return near the end of the sixth century BC.

In verses 8–40a, the author paints a detailed picture of idols as helpless, inanimate objects that are unable to do the simplest tasks for themselves (compare Isaiah 44:9–20 as well as the apocryphal book Bel and the Dragon). Since idols cannot help themselves, how can they benefit their worshipers?

Modern readers should understand that pagans often distinguished between the god and the idol that represented him or her. A carved or crafted idol would be infused with a power or presence of the pagan god at a ceremony. The idol would then serve as a focal point for the worshipers. Two things, however, should be noted. First, people could and did come to see the idol as something of an extension of the pagan god or goddess. In a way, it could be considered alive (as in Bel and the Dragon). Second, it was sacred to the god or goddess it represented and, as such, would be assumed to have the protection of the god and something of its power. Biblical and extra-biblical denunciations of idols highlight the folly of this whole system.

Verses 40b–73 turn the reader's attention from the idol to the idol worshiper, describing a practice forbidden to God's people: cultic prostitution. Verse 43 presents the sad situation of a woman who is chosen for sexual intercourse with a stranger at the pagan temple and then gives the woman who was left alone a hard time for not being chosen. What sort of upside-down morality brags about prostitution and elevates it above chastity? One rooted in idolatry rather than family. Lord, have mercy.

Verse 73 of this letter emphasizes the main point of the whole work: a just man, idol-less, bears none of the reproach heaped upon idol worshipers.

6 Susanna

You find yourself between a rock and a hard place, through no fault of your own. If you tell the truth, you most certainly will face terrible consequences. If you give in, you will commit a terrible sin but perhaps save your life. What are you going to do?

This short dramatic story describes a woman in this very situation. Modern readers will appreciate this "first detective story" as Susanna rejects the easy way out and chooses to remain faithful to the Lord.

Joakim, an exiled Jew living in Babylon, and his very beautiful wife, Susanna, are met first: two faithful children of God who knew the Scriptures and lived by them. You remember the villains of the story, two elders (civic leaders), who find themselves drawn to Susanna and begin to lust for her. The author points out (v. 9) that they could have fought this temptation by turning to heaven (God) or remembering righteous judgments (the Commandments and the Law). But they give in to their lust and plot together how they might accost her.

But the celebrated character is Daniel. Susanna is silent, possibly because women were not allowed to testify in court. The circumstantial evidence and the testimony of the respected community leaders would carry the day—they would condemn Susanna to death (v. 41). But she breaks her silence with a desperate plea for help from God, who moves Daniel to intervene.

Heroically, Daniel exposes the lie of the two villains in verses 47–63. Separating and interviewing them individually (a technique still used today), he shows that the two stories do not match. It may be helpful to note that God receives the credit for the outcome (v. 55).

The Book of Susanna demonstrates the wisdom of trusting God and following His commands, even at the risk of losing life itself. Nothing, not even survival, is worth disobeying God and denying your faith (see Luke 9:23–26).

Conclusion

The failure of the elders to combat temptation (v. 9) should alert us to the value of turning to the Lord and immersing ourselves in His Word whenever we face temptation to sin. When we follow the path of God's wisdom, we often face terrible risks, as did Susanna. When we follow Susanna's example—choosing God's way, even at the risk of our own lives—we will be okay, even if we would give up everything else in life. When we depart from the path of wisdom (as did Israel), the only solution is to repent and return in faith to the one true God. By the power and work of the Holy Spirit, we can learn from our folly and recommit to God's Word and kingdom (see Matthew 6:25–33). These great lessons of faith carried Israel out of exile and back into their homeland, and also prepared them for more terrible and even greater things to come.

These works attributed to Baruch, Jeremiah, and Daniel bridge us from the days of Israel's exile into those silent years between the Testaments, when prophets ceased to speak but Israel continued to work and pray and write. In our next session, we will meet another family in exile and explore the wisdom of the only writer in the Apocrypha whose real name we know.

Concluding Activities

Conclude the session with an appropriate prayer and distribute the study leaflet for week 2.

Gloriously Reveal the Works of God

Tobit; Ecclesiasticus 1:1–6:17

Preparing for the Session

Central Focus

All good gifts come from God (James 1:17), though God's people also experience suffering in this sin-broken world.

Objectives

That participants, led by the Holy Spirit working through God's Word, will

1. appreciate God's gifts and thank Him for them daily;
2. understand better the value of suffering for God's people; and
3. see the importance of wisdom and the third use of the Law as guides in daily life.

Note for the small-group leaders: Lesson notes and other materials you will need begin on page 57.

For the Lecture Leader

Session Plan

Worship

Begin the session with the hymn printed in the study leaflet. Accompaniments are available in denominational hymnals, such as *Lutheran Service Book* or *Lutheran Worship* (refer to hymnal index). (Note: Concordia Publishing House has available *The Concordia Organist.* All the initial worship hymns in the LifeLight courses are included in this resource. It's especially helpful for mission congregations and small parishes. See the list of study resources on p. 7.) Follow with this prayer:

Prayer

Father, grant us wisdom to know and do Your will. Help us to do this out of gratitude and love for You, not for selfish gain. By the gift of Your Spirit, enable us to deny ourselves daily and follow Your Son, our Savior and Lord, so that Your love for others shines brightly through us. Rescue us from every trial, strengthen us against every temptation, and deliver us from all evil. In Jesus' holy name. Amen.

Lecture Presentation

Introduction

Comic books offer readers a simple story with plenty of action and an eventual victory of good over evil. In their fictional world, they depend on a superhero to defeat the villain (usually a super-powerful enemy in his or her own right). In the struggle between good and evil, the comic book encourages its readers to imitate the hero and adopt similar positive virtues and ethics. For this week, you studied what might be called an early comic book, comical in some of its content and a comedy in which the Lord guides His people to a happy end.

1 Two Stories *(Tobit 1:1–20)*

In Tobit, two stories intertwine—that of Tobit, a middle-aged Israelite man living in Nineveh (near modern-day Mosul, Iraq), and that of Sarah, a young Israelite woman living with her parents in Ecbatana, Media (southeast of Nineveh, near modern-day Hamedan, Iran).

The author tells the story of these two pious and faithful Israelites as they face terrible challenges. Their piety, however, results in their rescue. The angel Raphael employs "superpowers" to free Sarah from the demon Asmodeus and cure Tobit of his blindness. Almsgiving (gifts to the righteous poor), tithing, prayer, proper care for aging parents, and burial of dead Israelites move God to bless Tobit and Sarah in accordance with the author's understanding of Deuteronomy 28–32. From the story, the reader understands that the road to similar blessings from the Lord is the path of piety and prayer modeled by Tobit and Sarah.

Historical and geographical details may indicate the author wanted his readers to understand the book was fictional. For example, Tobit says that he was a young man when Naphtali (and the other nine northern tribes) seceded from Jerusalem (Judah) in 1:4. He then adds that he was taken captive to Nineveh when the Assyrians conquered the northern ten tribes (Israel) and deported the population. Almost two hundred years passed between Israel's secession from Judah and Assyria's victory over Samaria, yet Tobit claims to have been a young man at the time of the secession and only middle-aged by the time of the deportation! So the work is obviously fictional.

The geography of Tobit offers a second hint that the book is fiction. Tobit's son, Tobias, travels southeast from Nineveh to Ecbatana to meet Sarah. Along the way, he stops by the banks of the Tigris River to wash his feet at the end of the first day and catches a fish (Tobit 6:2–4). This must have been a remarkable journey, since Nineveh sits on the east bank of the Tigris River. Thus, an eastern journey would never cross the Tigris, since the eastern bank of the Tigris served as the starting point of the journey. Such a glaring "error" would tell the reader that the book was not historical. The author makes his point with larger-than-life characters who live exemplary lives and are rewarded by rescue from God through a hero (Raphael) with "superpowers." If Israel imitated Tobit, they might receive a similar restoration.

Tobit lists the virtues his readers will want to adopt as their own:

- Unlike other northerners, he remained faithful to God by traveling to Jerusalem for sacrifices and festivals.
- He did not merely tithe (give 10 percent for the support of the priests); he triple-tithed, giving the third tithe to widows and orphans (compare James 1:27).
- He married within the extended family (see Genesis 26:34; 28:8, 9).
- He ate only kosher food, even in Gentile lands (as did Daniel in Daniel 1).
- He provided support for those in want (an act cited as a demonstration of faith in Matthew 25:31–46).
- He buried the Israelite dead (to remain unburied was a terrible thing, as reflected in Deuteronomy 21:23).

And yet, for all this, Tobit ends up broke and on the run from the law. Tobit teaches it is important for the believer to be willing to endure hardship in the short run for God's blessings in the long run. As we consider the story and teachings of Tobit, we will compare it with the stories and teachings in Scripture.

1 The Problems and Prayers of Tobit and Sarah *(Tobit 1:21–3:17)*

Like Job, Tobit loses all his wealth in the first stage of faith-testing (see Job 1:13–22). He loses his health and his social standing (see Job 2:7–8). Tobit's nephew supports him—until the nephew relocates. At that point, the family depends on Tobit's wife, Anna, for their support. Tobit unfairly accuses her of stealing a goat when she receives one as a bonus for her work. This prompts her to retort that all his charities and righteous deeds have achieved nothing for him (like Job's wife in Job 2:9).

Tobit's prayer (like the Book of Job) challenges the reader to answer the question "Why do the righteous suffer?" Like Job, Tobit does not accuse God of injustice, even though the reader might expect that. Rather, Tobit asks God to take him from this life and bring him to "the eternal abode" (3:6). Like others who find themselves tested to their extreme limits, Tobit longs for death and the peace that it brings (like Job in Job 3). Whereas Job pleaded his innocence of any wrongdoing, Tobit explains his suffering as the just punishment for his sins and the sins of his ancestors (Tobit 3:1–5). Job and Tobit may both ask the question "Why do the righteous suffer," but they answer it differently. For Tobit, human suffering is punishment from God for sin (Tobit 3:5). For Job, the answer is much more complex.

At this point, the author of Tobit introduces the second character of his book, Sarah. Her despair comes from seven unconsummated marriages and the reproach of her servants (as Tobit's wife had reproached him). Only her pious concern for her parents keeps her from committing suicide (Tobit 3:10) so, like Tobit and Job, she asks the Lord for the end of her life.

Intertestamental Judaism had a different view of women than does Holy Scripture (as we will see particularly in Ecclesiasticus). The modern reader may notice that Tobit's piety took two and a half chapters to describe, while Sarah's person and plight occupies only three verses. Like Abraham's wife, the Sarah of Tobit is childless, but for a different reason (the demon Asmodeus). Her piety consists of avoiding intimate contact with a man rather than a catalog of good deeds (Tobit 3:14), and her role in the story of Tobit is clearly minor compared to the men. In the final analysis, her faithfulness is defined by an exclusive relationship with Tobias and the promise of children from her union with him.

Tobit's author reveals a greater interest in angels and demons than Scripture, introducing the reader to Raphael (an angel of God's presence; 3:16) after mentioning the demon Asmodeus (3:8). Tobit's prayer, offered at the same time as Sarah's, results in God sending Raphael to heal Tobit and arrange the marriage of Tobias and Sarah.

2 Tobias's Journey *(Tobit 4–9)*

If Tobit's story reminds us of Job's, the story of Tobias's journey brings to mind the narrative of Jacob in Genesis 27–33. Both stories involve deception, travel, supernatural help, success, and unusual practices. Tobit uses the internal parts of the "miracle fish" to rescue both Sarah and Tobit from their predicaments.

A point of contrast between Tobit and canonical Scripture appears in the treatment of almsgiving (giving money to the poor and needy, a basic tenet of Jewish piety). Tobit's advice to Tobias seems a bit self-serving, as though the primary reason for helping others is to secure God's favor and assistance in time of need (Tobit 4:7–11). Tobit even restricts almsgiving to those who "live uprightly," or practice righteousness (4:7; see also 4:17).

Contrast with this the preaching of John the Baptist, who calls his followers to share with others without restriction (Luke 3:11). Or, consider the "Golden Rule" of Jesus (Matthew 7:12; see also Deuteronomy 15 and Ephesians 4:28). Acts of charity in canonical Scriptures serve to demonstrate saving faith (Matthew 25:31–46) and compassion (cf. Tabitha in Acts 9:36 and Cornelius in Acts 10:4). The primary difference between canonical Scripture and Tobit in their treatment of almsgiving is seen in the motivation behind charitable acts and the unrestricted scope of those to whom such gifts should be given. God's people give because they resemble their heavenly Father (Matthew 5:43–48), not as a hedge against future need (Tobit 4:9).

In Tobit 5, Raphael's deceptions present ethical problems for Christian readers but may have been understood as acceptable by the original audience in this fictional story. The author has made sure his readers know, by his historical and geographical notes, that this book is not a historical account of a real man and maiden. Like Abraham's encouragement to his servant who is sent to find a wife for Isaac (Genesis 24:7), Tobit assures Tobias of angelic assistance (5:17).

The burning of the fish's heart and liver are combined with ardent prayer to secure the defeat of the demon Asmodeus and the safety of Tobias (6:17–18). Readers may well recall the rebellion of Israel in Numbers 21:4–9 when God rescued His people from the fiery serpents with a bronze serpent. (The faith of those who looked to the bronze serpent is assumed in Numbers 21 and reflected in Jesus' use of it in John 3:14–15.) Following through on these instructions, Tobias and Sarah begin their marriage (Tobit 8:4–8).

3 The Homecoming *(Tobit 10–14)*

Like Jacob before him, Tobias returns with a wife and great wealth. He also returns with concern for his parents, knowing they were worried about him. The reader may ask, "If his father has faith (5:17–22), why does he struggle with doubt and worry (10:1–3)?" Like us, God's people throughout the ages often found themselves conflicted. Faith and unbelief inhabit the same heart, as was the case, for example, with the demon-possessed boy's father in Mark 9:24.

An old Latin phrase says it well: *Simul iustus et peccator*; we are "simultaneously justified and yet a sinner." The new man in Christ and the old Adam coexist in every child of God and create an internal conflict that continues throughout our entire life on earth. Tobit's struggle between trust and doubt may well have reflected the original audience's faith-struggle in the late third century BC or early second century BC. Gentiles still ruled them, poverty was still common, and no rescue seemed imminent. They may have struggled with the fact that God's timetable is often very different from ours, as Peter explained to his readers in 2 Peter 3. Tobit's story encourages them to stay the course and not falter from discouragement, for "the Lord will exalt His people" (14:7).

After testing, God restored Tobit to health, wealth, and social position. Tobit's restoration provided a model for his original readers, encouraging them to similar behavior in the hope of similar improvement.

Raphael reveals his true identity in 12:11–22. He explains that God sent him to help Tobit and Sarah because of Tobit's many good deeds. However, apart from Sarah's prayer, no note of Sarah's righteous acts appears, consistent with her relatively passive role in the narrative. Raphael's comments challenge the Christian reader to consider why God answers prayer.

Jesus teaches us to pray by addressing the almighty God as "Father" (Matthew 6:9; Luke 11:2), an intimate and warm family term. Luther "unpacks" this when he explains the introduction of the Lord's Prayer in his Small Catechism: "With these words God tenderly invites us to believe that He is our true Father and that we are His true children, so that with all boldness and confidence we may ask Him as dear children ask their dear father." In Tobit, the angel Raphael presents his prayers to God; in the Gospels, believers come directly to God in the name of Jesus (see John 16:23–26).

The author's hope for the restoration of Jerusalem and the temple comes to full expression in chapter 14 on the lips of Tobit. If God's people will walk in the path of righteousness and generosity (like Tobit), they will experience a blessed and glorious future (like Tobit).

Psalm 73 offers something of a necessary corrective to Tobit's formula for success. In that psalm, Asaph observes the wealth, respect, and easy life of evildoers. He admits that he wavered in his conviction to keep his focus exclusively on God (the "pure in heart" of v. 1, opposite of the "double-minded" in James 4:8). Every good gift comes from God (James 1:17), but it may please Him to distribute those gifts to those who disobey Him. Only at the final judgment do we see how the path of faith and righteousness is far superior to the way of unbelief and sinfulness, Asaph's point in Psalm 73:17. On earth, God's people may have to suffer and may struggle with doubt and unbelief. At the Last Day, however, God's people receive the inheritance won for them by Jesus (Hebrews 9:15; 1 Peter 1:4).

4 The Wisdom of Jesus Son of Sirach *(Ecclesiasticus 1:1–6:17)*

This Jesus from the Time between the Testaments presents a laundry list of topics. If you've read Proverbs, you've seen this before. His wisdom will round out our study today and occupy us for the next two sessions. Written in Hebrew between 200 and 175 BC, the Wisdom of Jesus son of Sirach (also known as Ecclesiasticus) offers advice on how to succeed in life. The Jewish people in Israel faced increasing pressure during these years to abandon the Jewish way of life in favor of the cosmopolitan culture passed down from Alexander the Great and his successors. Much like the Israelites who entered the Promised Land under Joshua twelve centuries earlier, the people of God needed to be warned against the paganism of the Gentiles living in the land. Jewish people who had moved away from Israel needed the same message. The path of wisdom that leads to success comes exclusively from obeying God's Word and adhering to the piety of their ancestors. Living in Egypt, the grandson of Jesus son of Sirach translated Ecclesiasticus into the common language of the day, Greek, so that all Jewish people could benefit from his grandfather's wisdom (see the Prologue).

This is the only book in the Apocrypha that bears the real author's name. Jesus son of Sirach offers his as a synthesis of Hebrew Scripture and his experiences from a lifetime of teaching and travel. Jesus son of Sirach's admonition to resist Greek religion and culture may have sounded hard enough to do when he wrote this book. But it would prove much more difficult in the years following, when Antiochus IV Epiphanes ruled (175–164 BC). The cost of the way of wisdom would get much higher.

Jesus son of Sirach begins by praising wisdom, and then he offers his first lesson to his students (2:1–6:17). Because the word *wisdom* is feminine in Hebrew, authors picture wisdom as a woman (Proverbs 8–9). Unlike Proverbs, Jesus son of Sirach understands wisdom as a created thing (Ecclesiasticus 1:9) rather than a personified attribute of God (as in Proverbs 8:22–31). As we know from the New Testament, Christ Jesus is the incarnate wisdom of God and the power of God (1 Corinthians 1:24). At the heart of wisdom for both Jesus son of Sirach and Holy Scripture is a right relationship with God, expressed as "the fear of the Lord," which is saving faith and faithful obedience (Ecclesiasticus 1:14; Psalm 111:10; Proverbs 9:10).

In chapter 3, Jesus son of Sirach affirms the duty owed to parents, one of the obligations emphasized by Tobit. The concepts of "honor" and "dishonor" may seem strange to modern Western readers, but they continue to play an important role in Eastern cultures. Western people might use the word "shame" to mean "embarrassment" but that is not what Eastern cultures have in mind. "Honor" would include social status, respect, and adherence to cultural values. "Shame" denotes failure and ultimately leads to exclusion and death. Isaiah, for example, points out that idol-makers will all be "put to shame" because their gods are a lie, promising help but failing to deliver (Isaiah 44:9–11). Similarly, Paul is not "ashamed" of the Gospel (Romans 1:16) because it actually does what it promises—saves us from eternal damnation.

"Humility" also can be easily misunderstood. The word translated "meekness" in Ecclesiasticus (3:17, ESV; "humility" NRSV) appears as a fruit of the Spirit in the New Testament (Galatians 5:23, "gentleness" NIV) and is a characteristic of Jesus (Matthew 11:29) and His followers (Matthew 5:5). It conveys a picture of someone who acts considerately toward others, with kindness and patience included. Jesus son of Sirach counsels his students to live with gentle consideration toward others (3:17–20, much like Paul's advice in 2 Timothy 2:25). James points out that this gentle consideration for others is closely linked to true wisdom (James 3:13).

Readers familiar with the New Testament will find many such parallels in Ecclesiasticus because both draw heavily from the Hebrew Scriptures, although we will see several stark differences as well.

Conclusion

During the period when Tobit and Ecclesiasticus were written, God's people in Judea must have often wondered what path would lead them back to the "glory days" of David and Solomon. The exiles who returned from Babylon under Persian rule (end of sixth to fifth century BC) had rebuilt the walls of Jerusalem and restored its temple. But it compared poorly to Solomon's glorious original. Following Alexander's conquest of the area and his death at the end of the fourth century BC, they found themselves under the rule of the Ptolemies. Life was hard and getting harder. Using a fictional story, the author of Tobit affirms that they suffer because they (and their ancestors) have sinned but that the path back to prosperity lay in scrupulous obedience to the Mosaic Law and the piety of their ancestors. Jesus son of Sirach offers the same advice, compiling a series of lessons on wisdom that paint the same picture: success lies at the end of the road of obedience to the Law and adherence to traditional piety.

In the next session, we will hear more from Jesus son of Sirach and learn more about how this Jesus differs from the one crucified and risen for our salvation. For now it is enough to say that the wisdom of these great books from the Time between the Testaments tells us much about life but not nearly enough about the life everlasting that the Lord promised throughout the Old Testament. One more faithful than Tobit was yet to come, whose suffering had the power to save. A wiser man than the son of Sirach was coming, whose words and works would stun the world and change our lives forever.

Concluding Activities

Conclude the session with an appropriate prayer and distribute the study leaflet for week 3.

The Lord's Great Mercy

Ecclesiasticus 6:18–33:19

Preparing for the Session

Central Focus

In the same way a travel guide might offer a tourist advice on making his way through a foreign country, Jesus son of Sirach instructs his students on how to successfully navigate through life, applying wisdom (especially the Word of God) to everyday living.

Objectives

That participants, led by the Holy Spirit working through God's Word, will

1. learn the nature and value of true wisdom in their lives;

2. appreciate that women were created in the image of God and that those who believe are co-heirs in Christ; and

3. rejoice in the promise of eternal life in Christ regardless of the circumstances and situations they face in this life.

Note for the small-group leaders: Lesson notes and other materials you will need begin on page 59.

For the Lecture Leader

Session Plan

Worship

Begin the session with the hymn printed in the study leaflet. Accompaniments are available in denominational hymnals, such as *Lutheran Service Book* or *Lutheran Worship* (refer to hymnal index). (Note: Concordia Publishing House has available *The Concordia Organist.* All the initial worship hymns in the LifeLight courses are included in this resource. It's especially helpful for mission congregations and small parishes. See the list of study resources on p. 7.) Follow with this prayer:

Prayer

Father, open our hearts and minds to Your Holy Spirit so that we might gain wisdom and understanding. Lift our eyes off this world to see You and find in Your Son, Jesus Christ, our Savior, the fullness of Your wisdom and power. Guide us so that we use our time wisely, living for You and the benefit of others. Fix our hearts on Jesus, the founder and perfecter of our faith. In His name. Amen.

Lecture Presentation

Introduction

"Get smart" we say in Western culture. We have learned to place value on critical thought and technology. Things were different in the ancient East; they would say, "Get wisdom!" and prize that above everything. This is something for us to consider as we continue with Jesus the son of Sirach. Wisdom plays an important role in the literature of the Middle Eastern cultures (including Israel) but appears less frequently in Western literature. Modern students of Scripture may not appreciate the breadth and depth of wisdom as taught in Scripture nor how it differs from worldly wisdom.

However, before we continue, we should acknowledge that Ecclesiasticus is a huge book, as you now know. Because the book returns again and again to similar themes, we will skip forward a bit in some places rather than cover every passage. So let us begin.

1 Wisdom

In the world, wisdom comes from experience. People live their lives and inevitably make mistakes. Learning from personal mistakes as well as successes, they pass along that information to the next generation. Since some people see things more clearly and can navigate the challenges of life more successfully, their advice is preserved and practiced. Such wisdom would include giving directives on advancing one's career, understanding the interrelation of cause and effect in the world, grasping the nature of politics and persuasion, and even applying scientific principles. In its highest form, wisdom considers the nature of good and evil and tries to address the problem of suffering and evil in the world. In short, worldly wisdom tries to make sense out of our environment and provide a guide for survival—and perhaps even success.

In the Bible, however, wisdom begins with God. Since God made the world and rules it, the beginning of wisdom is a right relationship with Him ("fear of the LORD" in Psalm 111:10; Proverbs 9:10). Because God reveals Himself and His will in Holy Scripture, real wisdom can be found only there (a favorite theme in Ecclesiasticus). Although "wisdom" in Scripture covers a gamut of practical skills, God's ultimate wisdom is the Messiah (Isaiah 11:2–3; 1 Corinthians 1:24).

In one key respect, Jesus son of Sirach's teaching on wisdom differs markedly from that of Holy Scripture in that Jesus son of Sirach offers no clear hope of eternal life. His wisdom offers guidance for this life only, although he hints at the possibility of some kind of life after death—such as 48:10–11, when he refers to Elijah's role as predecessor to the Messiah. (Similar is 44:16, which refers to Enoch who, like Elijah, did not suffer physical death.)

Paul, on the other hand, clearly links wisdom to eternal life through the Gospel of Jesus Christ (1 Corinthians 2:6–16). Such wisdom cannot be determined, Paul points out, by observation of the world or experience in life. True wisdom, the Gospel of Jesus Christ, must be revealed by God. And, once this wisdom is revealed and received by faith, it results in eternal life. From this new relationship, led by the Holy Spirit, the fruits of the new life appear (Galatians 5:22–23; Ephesians 1:16–18).

A second clear difference between Scripture and Jesus son of Sirach appears when the reader raises the issue of suffering. If wisdom leads inevitably to success because it operates in harmony with God's created order, then it must mean that people who suffer have angered God or acted foolishly. Thus, Job's friends assume his suffering follows some offense against God (since God always acts justly). The "mechanical" view of Job's friends (and Jesus son of Sirach) cannot answer the question "why do the righteous suffer and the wicked prosper?" Asaph affirms that the path of true wisdom does not necessarily lead to success in this world but to vindication on the day of judgment (Psalm 73). Even more surprising to those who would accept Jesus son of Sirach's wisdom is Scripture's revelation that some suffering exists for the sole purpose of glorifying God (resulting in saving faith) and is entirely unrelated to specific sins done by the sufferer (John 9:1–3). Suffering and hardship may even be God's work in the believer's life, refining faith and shaping one for service (1 Peter 1:3–9).

2 Wisdom, Women, and Kindness *(Ecclesiasticus 6:18–14:19)*

In 6:18–37, Jesus son of Sirach contemplates the difficulty of following the path of wisdom. Not only is human nature rebellious, rejecting God's way in favor of self-determination (see Genesis 3:1–6), but the path of wisdom also requires self-denial and strict self-discipline. This is especially hard for young people to do. Very few parents have children who have heeded their good advice and lived wisely at all times. Like a farm animal bearing a yoke (6:24–25), we may feel wisdom is overly restrictive. Only total devotion to wisdom can overcome the rebellious nature of humanity and the powerful urges of youth.

In chapter 7, Jesus son of Sirach affirms the old adage "You reap what you sow" (see Galatians 6:7). He reminds his readers that ambition should not lead them beyond their abilities to handle a situation. Worldly wise man Voltaire wrote that those who exercise great power must also exercise great responsibility. In general, Ecclesiasticus advises, treat other people fairly and fulfill your obligations. Its advice in 7:18 against exchanging a friend for money may help readers of the New Testament appreciate a little more the cultural violation that occurred when Judas betrayed Jesus (Matthew 26:15).

The subject of women in Ecclesiasticus 9:1–9 reveals an attitude in Jesus son of Sirach's work that differs sharply from Scripture. As a man of his own time and culture, he saw women as more of a threat and danger than modern Westerners may imagine. At this point in his work, Jesus son of Sirach simply warns against contact with the opposite sex. Even casual social contact could lead to inappropriate behavior (9:9). Daughters (7:24–25), wives (chs. 25–26), and other women (9:1–9) all create serious dangers for the man who seeks to follow the path of wisdom. Wayward daughters' behaviors may bring scandal and shame, destroying a man's honor. A wife can ruin a man's homelife (25:16–26); and even though a wife can be a blessing, the dangers inherent in women far outweigh the benefits (ch. 26). Given the very high standards imposed on women in Jesus son of Sirach's culture and the high value placed on honor, his remarks should not so greatly surprise the modern reader, nor are they as extreme as they may seem to Western people. A quick check of Sharia law on the role of women, or an explanation of why the burka is required for some Muslim women, confirms Jesus son of Sirach's view of women. We will look at Scripture's evaluation of women when we consider chapters 25 and 26 in a later session.

"Don't judge a book by its cover" and "Look before you leap" might well summarize chapter 11. The Lord Jesus uses an image similar to the figure in 11:18–19 when He tells the parable of the rich fool in Luke 12:16–21, regarding true wealth in God's eyes. The point our Lord makes in His parable is missing from Jesus son of Sirach's writing, although Ecclesiasticus does call for responsible use of wealth (14:3–19).

Jesus son of Sirach's advice in 12:4–6 seems at odds with our Lord Jesus' directive to do good to everyone (Luke 6:32–36). However, the difference between their teachings may not be as great as it first appears. The Lord Jesus teaches kindness to all, but Jesus son of Sirach teaches that believers should show kindness but not extend it so far as to become involved in the life and plans of the ungodly. Believers who do so may find themselves trapped in a web of entanglement from which escape is impossible. The Lord Jesus speaks from a concern for all people, while Jesus son of Sirach teaches from a perspective of self-interest and self-preservation. For our Lord Jesus, life is all about serving God by blessing other people, even though it may involve a certain level of risk. Jesus son of Sirach wants to chart a course through the rocky shoals of life with minimal risk to the traveler. The same concern extends through chapter 13.

3 Wisdom and the Fall into Sin *(Ecclesiasticus 14:20–20:31)*

Jesus son of Sirach affirms God's goodness in 15:11–20, reminding the reader that God leads no one astray (cf. James 1:13). Scripture would agree that Adam and Eve had a real choice between good and evil but would disagree with Jesus son of Sirach that fallen humanity possesses a free will ("possible not to sin"; *posse non peccare*). Since the fall (Genesis 3:1–6), human beings can choose only sin and rebellion, as Paul summarizes in Romans 1:18–3:30 ("not possible not to sin"; *non posse non peccare*). Even the Christian must fight against the old, sinful nature on a daily basis (Romans 7). Only after we have entered our heavenly home will we be free of this bondage of the will ("not possible to sin"; *non posse peccare*).

Jesus son of Sirach offers examples of God's justice in the past, such as the punishment of the Nephilim, or "giants," of Genesis 6; Sodom and the other cities of Genesis 19; and the Canaanites in Joshua's conquest of Canaan. These examples support his argument that no sin will go unpunished by God. Unlike the writers of Scripture, Jesus son of Sirach does not place this divine justice in the context of a final judgment, either at the end of an individual's life (see Psalm 73) or at the end of time (see Matthew 26:31–46).

In 16:24–17:24, Jesus son of Sirach points to the design and smooth operation of nature as evidence for wisdom's efficiency and attention to detail. He encourages his students to live in harmony with this design and to fulfill their destiny, praising God and proclaiming His glory (17:10). To those who have lived in rebellion against God's design and will, he encourages repentance in the hope that the Lord will show mercy (17:25–32).

Like Moses in Psalm 90, Jesus son of Sirach considers the brevity of human life in the context of God's power and sovereignty (18:1–14). Like Isaiah in chapter 55 (especially vv. 9–10), Jesus son of Sirach recognizes the Lord's compassion for His people and His interest in returning them to Himself. Because God so graciously provides for His people, His people need to help others in the same spirit (18:15–18).

"Look before you leap" might also capture the spirit of 18:19–29. Wisdom slows down a person's reactions, lifting eyes off the immediate circumstances to see the larger context and the consequence of every decision. The wise person considers God's negative response to unfulfilled promises (vows) and hastens to do what he has promised to do before facing God on the last day of life. Unlike the psalmist who penned Psalm 130, Jesus son of Sirach does not direct his students to the mercy of the Lord or the forgiveness that lies at the heart of our relationship with God.

An admonition to self-control (18:30–19:3) and a warning against gossip (19:4–17) continue Jesus son of Sirach's "keys to success" approach. New Testament authors also address these issues (Ephesians 4:17–32; James 3:1–12), but they differ from Jesus son of Sirach in anchoring their advice in the Gospel (with a genuine concern for others). This contrasts with Jesus son of Sirach's focus on self-preservation and advancement. The remainder of chapters 19 and 20 extend Jesus son of Sirach's teaching on the need for careful, prudent, and honest speech in the life of a person who follows the path of wisdom.

4 Genuine Wisdom in Israel *(Ecclesiasticus 21:1–27:29)*

Wise and foolish people reveal their natures as they interact with others socially (21:11–28). Jesus son of Sirach uses vivid metaphors. For example, he writes about "a mind . . . like a broken jar" (v. 14), and he makes wordplays on "cleverness" (v. 12) and "mouth/heart" (v. 26). Jesus son of Sirach contrasts wise and foolish social behavior. He portrays the fool as speaking without thought or sensitivity to the impact on others. The wise man exercises caution, thinking about what he says before he speaks. St. Paul offers similar counsel when he urges his readers to use the gift of language wisely, glorifying God and building up other Christians (Ephesians 4:15–20).

Jesus son of Sirach picks up the theme of the slothful individual (22:1–2) and moves immediately to write about children who disappoint their parents (22:3–8). His comment on daughters (v. 3b) may seem harsh to modern readers, but it reflects the economic burden incurred at the birth of a daughter in that culture. A son would remain in the larger family and provide an additional source of income. A daughter would marry and leave the family, costing her father a dowry in the process (see 1 Kings 9:16 and 2 Maccabees 1:14). Socially, it was important that a daughter please her husband, but sons faced no such expectations regarding their wives. A daughter was much more expensive than a son and represented a much higher risk of incurring shame.

In 22:9–18, Jesus son of Sirach once again contrasts wisdom and folly. He humorously compares gluing a broken pot together with teaching a fool (v. 9). In the same vein, almost everyone can relate to 22:15, which perhaps reflects Jesus son of Sirach's reading of Proverbs 27:3. Christians will want to remember that even stupid people matter to God and offer an opportunity to show kindness (consider the "Golden Rule" in Matthew 7:12).

After discussing the limits and benefits of friendship (22:19–26), Jesus son of Sirach offers a prayer resembling David's Psalm 141 (22:27–23:15). Like James (James 3:1–12), Jesus son of Sirach recognizes the challenge of controlling the tongue and extends his prayer to include thoughts and desires. It's important for God's children to realize that in the battle against sin, the first front is in the mind. For example, Eve engaged temptation with her eyes and her mind before yielding to sin (Genesis 3:1–6). David did the same with Bathsheba (2 Samuel 11). Jesus shows us the way to successfully engage the enemy in our mind, by using Holy Scripture (Matthew 4; Luke 4).

The people of God often find themselves at odds with their own culture. In chapter 24, Jesus son of Sirach argues that true wisdom made her home in Israel—not of her own choice but because God chose her home (v. 8). He identifies true wisdom with "the book of the covenant"; that is, Holy Scripture. In the second century BC, God's people faced intense pressure to Hellenize, to adopt the culture, dress, language, and religion of the Greeks. Sophisticated, educated, and progressive, Greek culture seemed superior in every way to Judaism and its traditions. Yet Jesus son of Sirach wants his students to know that real wisdom (the Scriptures) dwelt in Jewish culture at God's direction. He encourages his readers to remain faithful to their heritage. The writers of the New Testament make a similar point when directing readers to the ultimate wisdom of God, who sent Jesus Christ to make His dwelling among us and bring salvation to the world (see John 1:1–18).

In 25:1–26:18, Jesus son of Sirach contemplates the contrast between a good wife and an evil one. (Note how the negative far outweighs the positive in his account.) Proverbs will also remark on the challenge of living with a contentious spouse (19:13; 21:9; 27:15) but spends much more time praising the virtuous wife than complaining about a difficult one (18:22; 31:10–31). While the "good wife" of Jesus son of Sirach is very passive (Ecclesiasticus 26:13–18), the godly wife of Proverbs is very active in her faith—she buys the household necessities, produces goods, manages the servants, supervises the fields, trades profitably, extends charity to the needy, keeps her family well-clothed and warm, works hard, acts with dignity, and speaks with wisdom. The godly wife of Scripture is a well-rounded human being and an admirable servant of the living God in her own right.

5 Wisdom and Selflessness *(Ecclesiasticus 27:30–33:19)*

Interpersonal relationships serve as the subject matter for chapters 28 and 29. Some of what Jesus son of Sirach teaches finds parallels in the New Testament. For example, the standard we use for judging others will be used to judge us (compare 28:1 with Matthew 7:2), and receiving forgiveness directly connects to forgiving others (compare 28:2 with Matthew 6:14–15). At other times, his advice and the Lord Jesus' call to radical discipleship clash (compare 29:1–13 with Luke 6:34–35). Note how

Jesus son of Sirach continues to teach with self-benefit as the priority, whereas our Lord Jesus teaches from a different perspective about reckless love, a concern for the other person that overrides one's own welfare—an approach that He Himself modeled at the cross.

Jesus son of Sirach's advice concerning children contrasts sharply with Scripture but has some common concerns. Both value discipline (as in Proverbs 13:24; 22:15), but Jesus son of Sirach's advice seems far more harsh, both in the severity of the discipline and in the withholding of affection (see 30:9–10). Contrast the tone of Proverbs 4, where the son remembers fondly his father's instruction concerning wisdom. The negative approach of Jesus son of Sirach reflected in his comments on women and the general tone of his instruction, emphasizing what to avoid rather than what to pursue, appears again in chapter 30 regarding sons.

Jesus son of Sirach's reference to "eternal rest" in 30:17 should not be understood in the same way as "rest" in Matthew 11:29. In Scripture, "eternal rest" refers to a continuous conscious life with God without any of the burdens or sorrows of this life (as in Revelation 7:15–17; 21:3–4). In Ecclesiasticus 31:17, "rest" refers only to a cessation of life and the activities that go along with life; it parallels "death" in the preceding line.

When Jesus son of Sirach considers the subject of election, God's decision about people before they are born, he does so without the benefit of the cross. Without the love of God displayed in Christ crucified for the sins of the whole world, the sovereignty of God can easily terrify a person. Both Jesus son of Sirach and St. Paul use the figure of a potter with clay to teach the sovereignty of God (Ecclesiasticus 33:13; Romans 9:20–24), but Paul always looks at this doctrine through the lens of the cross (see Ephesians 1:1–14). Scripture teaches an election to eternal life through Jesus Christ for all who believe, but it never teaches a "double predestination," where some are destined for damnation without hope for eternal life. Nor does it teach a "limited atonement," where Christ died for some, not all. Additionally, Jesus son of Sirach considers only a person's station in this life rather than the person's eternal destiny.

Conclusion

Chapters 6–33 of Ecclesiasticus show us many points of agreement with Scripture generally and with the New Testament as well. However, we also see that the son of Sirach taught self-preserving wisdom that warned against the dangers in life while failing to teach the compassion so characteristic of Jesus Christ. Should this surprise us? Not really. If you believe in free will so that life is what you make it, if you believe there is no life after this one so that you have to make the most of this life now, then naturally the risky, self-sacrificing wisdom of Jesus Christ will seem extreme.

However, if you are a sinner overwhelmed by your sins, if you have stumbled and failed in this life, then the wisdom of Jesus Christ is like no other—a wisdom that not only preserves but saves.

Concluding Activities

Conclude the session with an appropriate prayer and distribute the study leaflet for week 4.

The Blessed Fear the Lord

Ecclesiasticus 33:20–51:30

Preparing for the Session

Central Focus

Jesus son of Sirach guides travelers on the journey of life by celebrating the God-blessed accomplishments of earlier believers.

Objectives

That participants, led by the Holy Spirit working through God's Word, will

1. grow to love other people, including their enemies, as God loves them;
2. praise God, the creator and sustainer of the universe; and
3. praise God, the author and director of the plan of salvation that finds its fulfillment in Jesus Christ.

Note for the small-group leaders: Lesson notes and other materials you will need begin on page 61.

For the Lecture Leader

Session Plan

Worship

Begin the session with the hymn printed in the study leaflet. Accompaniments are available in denominational hymnals, such as *Lutheran Service Book* or *Lutheran Worship* (refer to hymnal index). (Note: Concordia Publishing House has available *The Concordia Organist*. All the initial worship hymns in the LifeLight courses are included in this resource. It's especially helpful for mission congregations and small parishes. See the list of study resources on p. 7.) Follow with this prayer:

Prayer

Thank You, Father, for the gift of Your Word, Holy Scripture. Help us learn wisdom from Your Word and follow the example of those who served You faithfully in the past. Guide us by Your Holy Spirit to reflect the light of true wisdom, Jesus Christ, in all we say and do. Preserve us from all evil and lead us through all trial and temptation. In Jesus' name. Amen.

Lecture Presentation

Introduction

The father is not even dead yet, and his son asks for his share of the inheritance! So Jesus begins His famous parable of the prodigal son (Luke 15:11–32). In contrast, Jesus son of Sirach's advice is markedly more conservative: keep your property until you pass it on as an inheritance on the day of your death (33:20–24).

When we read the Lord Jesus' parable in light of Jesus son of Sirach's teaching, we can appreciate just how shocking the New Testament story would have been. By comparing these two teachings, we see once again the value of studying the Time between the Testaments, which gives us that crucial background we need for rightly understanding the Lord's teaching.

1 Slavery and Empire *(Ecclesiasticus 33:20–36:31)*

Regarding slaves (33:25–33), Jesus son of Sirach's advice reflects the same harsh attitude he displayed toward children and women that we saw in earlier sessions. He counsels unremitting hard work for the slave and torture if the slave fails to perform to expectations. Although the teaching of 33:31–33 seems less harsh, the apparent kindness arises only from selfish considerations. A man with only one slave depends on that slave for everything. Since the owner could afford only one slave, he likely cannot afford to replace him if he runs away. So, reasonable treatment of the slave will assure his continued loyalty—a completely self-centered motivation.

In the ancient world, slavery had no racial overtones, as it does in much of the Western world today. A person might become a slave for a variety of reasons: one could be born into slavery, taken captive in battle, remiss in paying off debts, or enslaved for the sake of daily bread in difficult times. Scripture commands slave owners to treat their slaves with kindness (Ephesians 6:9) and at times to free them (Philemon 15–16). The Bible clearly condemns the slave trade toward the end of the New Testament (1 Timothy 1:10; Revelation 18:13).

Jesus son of Sirach next condemns the variety of ways people search for wisdom, all in vain (34:1–8). Only the Law of the Lord (the Hebrew Scriptures) offers wisdom. Although the Lord sometimes uses dreams and visions, He most often He does not send us such dreams and visions—much less omens and divinations (see Deuteronomy 18:9–14). Instead, God sends prophets to communicate with His people (Deuteronomy 18:15–22).

As Jesus son of Sirach's topics make clear, he enjoyed a fairly high social position. In 34:9–13, he even talks about the value of travel, something only fairly wealthy people could do. As is often the case today, travel to a distant land involves a certain level of risk. Thus, the wise man not only expands his worldview but learns survival skills.

The prayer in Ecclesiasticus 36:1–22 arises out of a situation of foreign domination. God's people who lived in Israel had returned from exile under Persian domination, which had continued until Alexander's conquest. Since then, they had not only lived under Gentile rulers but had also faced increasing pressure to "go Greek." The animosity toward non-Jews that appears in this prayer flows from centuries of bondage under non-believers. The next several centuries saw terrible persecution of the Jewish faith and a Roman takeover of the land so that these feelings of anger against foreigners did not diminish at all. This helps explain the reaction of the crowd at Nazareth in Luke 4:14–30. Like the son of Sirach, they expected the Lord Jesus to promise the destruction of the hated Gentiles. Instead, He pointed out the faith of two Gentiles as models for God's own people (Naaman the Syrian and the widow of Zarepath). No wonder the people in the synagogue tried to kill Him! In Matthew 5:43–48, the Lord Jesus explains His approach to foreigners and challenges us to the same love for them.

2 Life's Advantages *(Ecclesiasticus 37:1–39:11)*

"A friend in need is a friend indeed." This is an old saying that summarizes Jesus son of Sirach's comments in 37:1–6. Only in times of adversity do we know our real friends, as Jesus son of Sirach notes, "In the face of battle take up the shield" (37:5b). The Scriptures reveal our greatest Friend who not only "takes up the shield" but lays down His life for us—Jesus Christ (John 15:12–17). Most people will develop friendships with others who are like them (expressed in the adage "Birds of a feather flock together"). Not so Jesus. Even though He is God Incarnate, He reaches out to all people, becoming a "friend of tax collectors and sinners" (Matthew 11:19).

In Ecclesiasticus 37:7–15, Jesus son of Sirach even gives advice on people who give advice. Scripture records several instances of bad advice that sometimes produced unwanted results. For example, when Rehoboam inherited the kingdom of Israel from his father, he had to decide whether to lower the taxes (as the elders advised) or increase them (as friends advised). He followed the advice of his friends, and the northern ten tribes rebelled and picked a different king (1 Kings 12). What is more, even good advisers can give bad advice. Nathan the prophet gave David a green light when he asked about building a temple for God (2 Samuel 7). He had to reverse himself the next day after God corrected him. Godly friends and a heart informed by Scripture make excellent advisers but, as Jesus son of Sirach points out, the very best adviser is God Himself. When we need direction, we first take it to the Lord in prayer and await His answer (see Proverbs 3:5–6; Psalm 37:5–7).

The advice in Ecclesiasticus 37:27–31 might be summarized as "Find what you really like, but don't overdo it." Consistent with all of Jesus son of Sirach's teaching, the advice reflects a self-centered approach to life that conflicts with the other-centered ethic found in Scripture. Our Lord Jesus, for example, directs His students to focus on the kingdom of God and the life-practices that flow from that rather than the "stuff" of this life (Matthew 6:25–34).

Ecclesiasticus 38:1–15 highlights a tension that often challenges God's people today. When faced with illness, do we seek relief from physicians and pharmacists or from God in prayer? Jesus son of Sirach and James would say "both" (see James 5:14–15; oil was regarded as medicinal, as in Luke 10:34). Western medicine looks at disease from a purely physical perspective, often ignoring the spiritual and psychological components. At the other extreme, some people avoid doctors and medicines entirely, depending on prayer alone for healing. Both see only part of the picture. People are body and soul, mind and spirit. Illness involves the whole person. The best approach, as advised by James, places God at the center and utilizes both prayer and medical help. Ultimately, all healing comes from the Great Physician Himself, whether through the means of doctors and drugs or directly by God (cf. Mark 5:25–34).

Even grieving should be done in moderation (38:16–23), according to the son of Sirach, and with a sensitivity to social response (avoiding criticism, 38:17c). How different the consolation of Scripture! For example, St. Paul reminds us of the wonderful future all believers have through faith in Christ—spiritual life with Him from the moment of our death until we are raised from the dead on the Last Day to reign with Him in everlasting glory (1 Thessalonians 4:13–18; 1 Corinthians 15; see also Jesus' remarks to the dying man in Luke 23:43).

In Ecclesiasticus 38:24–39:11, Jesus son of Sirach highlights the advantages of his own profession: an expert in the Hebrew Scriptures, including its interpretations and applications by previous teachers. He acknowledges the value of the trades that make life possible (especially the time necessary for professional scribes to develop their skills). But he praises the work of the lawyer above all. Scribes were known as "lawyers" because they rendered binding decisions based on the Law of Moses and previous rulings. They began as copyists, becoming familiar with Scripture one letter at a time. Since they knew the text better than anyone else, they were often asked to convey its meaning and apply it to the lives of their contemporaries. By the time of our Lord Jesus' public ministry, the scribes had become guardians and caretakers of an approach to Scripture that failed to see the "big picture"; that is, God's mercy and our treatment of other people (Matthew 9:13; 12:7). As a group, they rejected the Lord Jesus. Yet wise scribes would recognize Jesus as the Messiah and take to heart His corrections (see Matthew 23).

3 Living in the Present *(Ecclesiasticus 39:12–42:14)*

The son of Sirach's hymn of praise declares God's complete rule over creation. Yet the fact that people have the power to make some choices themselves doesn't seem to be addressed. In the ancient world, philosophers thought that world events and the lives of individuals could be understood either as luck or as fate. In contrast, the New Testament would answer that God directs all things for the purpose of saving people from eternal damnation (see Romans 8:28–39). Jesus son of Sirach provides a somewhat different answer: good things for good people, evil things for sinners (39:25). Those who choose wisdom receive blessings from the Lord, but those individuals and nations who turn away from God find God's good gifts a problem and receive punishment from God through natural disasters.

At the end of Jesus son of Sirach's hymn of praise, he concludes that God provides aid at the right time and, since everything ultimately has a good purpose, the proper response is praise and thanksgiving (39:33–35). Scripture would agree. Because God alone is good, every good gift we have necessarily comes from Him (James 1:17), and our appropriate response is thanksgiving (Psalm 107:1; 118:1, 29; 136) and a life of sacrificial obedience (Romans 12:1).

Ecclesiasticus 41:1–14 contains Jesus son of Sirach's contemplation of death and the legacy people leave behind when they are gone. In agreement with Scripture, the son of Sirach understands that the end of life brings with it the end of all activity in this age, even the worship of God and the study of His Word (cf. Psalm 6, especially v. 5). Wise people leave a legacy of wise children and a good reputation. Foolish people leave a heritage of troubled offspring and infamy. As the "great equalizer," death comes to all men—welcomed by the suffering and dreaded by the successful (somewhat similar to what Solomon said in Ecclesiastes, especially in ch. 9). The broader view of Scripture looks past this somewhat earth-bound perspective to the life we have with God, which continues beyond the grave. God, a God of the living (see Matthew 22:31–32), keeps alive those who die in faith and raises them on the Last Day for life in a new world (Isaiah 65:17; 66:22; 2 Peter 3:13; Revelation 21:1). God works in this age to bring people to saving faith in Jesus Christ so that they rise to life, not to judgment, on that day. The sufferings of God's people in this age serve the purpose of bringing the Gospel to lost sinners, a benefit more than worth the pain and struggle involved (affirmed by Paul in Romans 8:18–39).

4 Praise for God and Men *(Ecclesiasticus 42:15–46:20)*

The section of 42:15–43:33 comprises a four-part hymn of praise from nature (42:15–25), things we see when we look up (sun, moon, and rainbow; 43:1–12), weather systems (snow, hail, and mist; 43:13–27); and finally the Creator Himself (43:28–33). Like the author of Psalm 104, Jesus son of Sirach sees the glory of God revealed at least in the world that God created and maintains. Anyone who looks around at the world should conclude that (1) God is one; (2) God's power is displayed in His creation; and (3) people should worship Him (see Romans 1:18–23).

Jesus son of Sirach acknowledges that God is far greater than His creation, of which we see only a small part (43:32–33). Pantheism, the teaching that God is the sum of the universe, is not reflected in 43:27. There, Jesus son of Sirach summarizes his praise of God as creator and sustainer of the universe: "He is the all." Like St. Paul, Jesus son of Sirach would confess that all of creation finds its origin and existence in God but that He is far greater than all of creation—He is Lord and ruler of all (see 1 Corinthians 15:28). Unlike Jesus son of Sirach, St. Paul would add that we find the fullness of creation in the person of Jesus Christ, Head of the Church, in whom creation is fully restored (see Ephesians 1:22–23). We have this now in part, and we look forward to the day when we will live under a new heaven on a new earth (see 1 Corinthians 13:12–13).

In chapter 44, Jesus son of Sirach begins a hymn of praise to men who embody the ideals of wisdom taught in the previous chapters of his book. Note: there are no women in the list. Christians may notice a sharp contrast between the general picture painted by Jesus son of Sirach and the utter poverty of wisdom Incarnate, Jesus Christ (cf. 44:6; Isaiah 52:13–53:12; Matthew 8:20). Jesus son of Sirach does admit that some who practiced wisdom went unnoticed in their lifetimes but produced deeds that are remembered (44:8–11).

In his hymn, Jesus son of Sirach postpones mention of Adam, who followed the lead of his wife, Eve, in the Garden (Genesis 3:1–6). Instead, he begins the story of salvation with Enoch (44:16; he appears again in 49:14–16 along with Adam). The son of Sirach's interest in the priestly line becomes obvious when he writes about Aaron (45:6–22) and the lengthy description of Simon son of Onias, who was high priest at the time (50:1–21). For Jesus son of Sirach, God's salvation history moves forward in the high priests, descendants of Levi and Aaron.

Readers of the New Testament may not appreciate the problem presented by a Judean Messiah rather than one descended from Levi. Only a descendant of Levi could offer a sacrifice, according to Mosaic Law. How then could the Lord Jesus, a descendant of Judah, offer Himself as the perfect sacrifice for sin? Scripture answers by pointing to a priesthood superior to that of Levi and Aaron, the priesthood of Melchizedek. Since Abraham (the lesser) tithed to Melchizedek (the greater), Abraham's descendants, subordinate to Melchizedek (the point of verse 4 of Davidic Psalm 110). This is further spelled out in Hebrews 5–7 (cf. Genesis 14:18–20). Thus, Jesus, a descendant of Judah, can offer a legitimate sacrifice for sin as a priest in the order of Melchizedek.

At the heart of Jesus son of Sirach's hymn of praise to these men is their devotion to the Law of God (such as Abraham; 44:19–20a). The author of Hebrews has a somewhat similar list but points to the faith of those on the list, not their adherence to the Law. Significantly, those who lived by faith did not receive their inheritance on earth but looked beyond the grave to eternal life with God (Hebrews 11:1–2, 16, 39–40).

The priestly garments of Aaron feature prominently in Jesus son of Sirach's treatment of Moses' brother (Ecclesiasticus 45:6–22). (A description of these garments with notes can be found in *The Apocrypha: The Lutheran Edition with Notes*, pp. 132–33.) Contrast the appearance of our great High Priest, Jesus Christ, at the time of His sacrifice on the cross. Numbers 25 records the story of Phinehas, grandson of Aaron through Eleazar. Jesus son of Sirach pauses in his praise of Phinehas to pray for the high priest of his time, Simon II, "embedded" in his ancestor (Ecclesiasticus 45:26).

5 Kings and Rulers *(Ecclesiasticus 47–51)*

When Jesus son of Sirach evaluates Solomon (47:12–22), he includes a section of harsh criticism concerning Solomon's many wives. Consistent with the son of Sirach's warnings throughout his book, the women led Solomon astray. They stained his honor, defiled his posterity, and divided the kingdom (see 1 Kings 11). The defiling of his posterity is demonstrated in his son Rehoboam, who ignored the advice of older counselors and followed the foolish advice of his friends, resulting in the loss of the northern ten tribes (1 Kings 12).

The section on Elijah (48:1–11) contains the strongest evidence that Jesus son of Sirach believed in some sort of life after death (see v. 11). Elijah ascended into heaven by means of a whirlwind (2 Kings 2:11). A chariot of fire separated Elijah and his protégé, Elisha, but Jesus son of Sirach combines the two things (48:9). The biblical text does not say that Elijah rode the chariot but that the whirlwind took Elijah to heaven. Since God's presence is manifested by a whirlwind in Job (38:1; 40:6), we should see a picture of God Himself taking Elijah to heaven. From there, Elijah will come to proclaim the advent of the messianic King (Ecclesiasticus 48:10; Malachi 4:5). Jesus son of Sirach does not explain why those who saw Elijah and fell asleep in love will live somehow after death.

Simon II, the son of Onias, served as high priest from 219–196 BC. Jesus son of Sirach describes Simon's participation in a liturgical event (ch. 50). The blessing he pronounced at the end of the service was most likely the Aaronic benediction still used today (Numbers 6:22–27).

Jesus son of Sirach closes his work with a prayer of praise to God for deliverance (51:1–12) and a short poem about wisdom (51:13–30).

Conclusion

Throughout his work, Jesus son of Sirach draws from Holy Scripture, his culture, and his personal experience to put together a practical work that will help his students navigate the difficult and dangerous waters of life. We find many similarities between his work and other works of wisdom in Scripture (Ecclesiastes, Proverbs, Job, and others), but the differences overshadow the similarities. For example, Scripture teaches a Savior, a Redeemer who will raise us to life on the Last Day (such as in Job 19:25–27).

Jesus son of Sirach also supported the freedom of the will (against the biblical doctrine of the bondage of the will). He held a harsh attitude toward women and slaves. We might also note the comparative lack of compassion on the part of Jesus son of Sirach toward the lower classes and a consistent concern for the self. How different the attitude of Jesus, who was a friend of tax collectors and sinners!

Although Christians in the past and in the present could find good advice on numerous topics in this work, we can also see why neither the rabbis nor the earliest Christians considered it the Word of God.

Concluding Activities

Conclude the session with an appropriate prayer and distribute the study leaflet for week 5.

Additions to Holy Scripture

Old Greek Esther; Prayer of Manasseh; Prayer of Azariah; The Song of the Three Holy Children; Bel and the Dragon

Preparing for the Session

Central Focus

Even though the Bible might not answer every question we have or doesn't include information about something we wish it did, the Holy Spirit inspired the text to fulfill God's good purposes for His Church.

Objectives

That participants, led by the Holy Spirit working through God's Word, will

1. learn that God is always at work "behind the scenes" for the salvation of people;
2. know that, even in the midst of the crucible of suffering, God is with them; and
3. appreciate the worthlessness of false gods and thus keep faith with the one true God.

Note for the small-group leaders: Lesson notes and other materials you will need begin on page 63.

For the Lecture Leader

Session Plan

Worship

Begin the session with the hymn printed in the study leaflet. Accompaniments are available in denominational hymnals, such as *Lutheran Service Book* or *Lutheran Worship* (refer to hymnal index). (Note: Concordia Publishing House has available *The Concordia Organist.* All the initial worship hymns in the LifeLight courses are included in this resource. It's especially helpful for mission congregations and small parishes. See the list of study resources on p. 7.) Follow with this prayer:

Prayer

Father, pour out Your Holy Spirit into our hearts to open our eyes so that we can see Your hand moving events in the world and in our lives toward salvation and hope. Help us always to trust You, even when we don't see the end of the problems we face. Teach us that You are always with us and that You are working all things for good in our lives and in the world. In Jesus' name. Amen.

Lecture Presentation

Introduction

Revelation, the last book of the Bible, warns readers against adding to or subtracting from its prophecies:

> I warn everyone who hears the words of the prophecy of this book: if anyone adds to them, God will add to him the plagues described in this book, and if anyone takes away from the words of the book of this prophecy, God will take away his share in the tree of life and in the holy city, which are described in this book. (22:18–19)

But it was not always so. At least that is what we find in the Time between the Testaments. A number of writers chose to add to biblical books rather than write their own. Or perhaps they added in a poem that someone else wrote because, well, it just fit so perfectly into the story.

For this session, you've read from a number of these additions to the Bible. Let us consider why people at this time tried to enhance the Bible as they knew it. An obvious reason would be that the existing book would lend credibility to the newly added words. What better way to get your message out than to piggyback on someone else's authority? A second motive was that sometimes a book of the Bible didn't seem to say everything it should. Let's face it, the Hebrew edition of the Book of Esther sure could use at least one mention of God. The writer or writers who added to Esther likely felt they were adding finishing touches, better drama, and a happier ending.

In defense of these writers, one might point out that the boundaries of what we call the Old Testament weren't entirely settled in their day. They may have seen themselves improving a good book before it became *the* Good Book. Whatever the case, they were uniquely successful in making their enlarged versions widely used. Although scribes have always felt tempted to add and embellish the books they worked on, few did so with greater success than the scribes who worked in the Time between the Testaments. Let's take a closer look at their impressive work.

1 Old Greek *(Esther 11:2–13:18)*

The biblical Book of Esther provides the background for the Jewish festival of *Purim*, "Lots," referring to the casting of lots (Esther 9:26–29). It is a story of how God saves His people from a terrible massacre simply because He cares for them.

Written sometime in the late fifth or first half of the fourth centuries BC, biblical Esther takes place in the ancient city of Susa (modern-day southwestern Iran, near the border with Iraq). At the time of biblical Esther, Susa was a major city in the Persian empire. After Alexander the Great conquered the area (ca. 331 BC), Susa's importance diminished greatly. It's helpful to remember that Alexander was from Macedon, a kingdom on the northern edge of Greece, rather than from one of the central Greek city-states such as Thebes or Athens. This explains why the author(s) of Old Greek Esther changed the nationality of the "bad guy" in the story to make him a Macedonian meddling in Persian politics.

These additions to Esther "update" the book to make the story more relevant to the audience of the early second century BC. Not only do the additions explicitly mention God, but they also revise Mordecai and Esther, turning them into examples of how faithful Jewish people live under foreign rule. The additions also serve to draw a distinct line between faithful Jews and pagan Gentiles, reinforcing the "us/them" mentality so prominent in the world of Jesus' ministry and the early Church's struggles (such as the Jerusalem Decree in Acts 15). Adding the full text of various proclamations gives the impression of authority and accuracy to the additions.

The additions at the beginning and end of Esther provide "bookends" for the story of Esther (additions A and F, chapters 11:2–12:6 at the beginning and 10:4–11:1 at the end). If Mordecai had indeed been among the captives taken to Babylon by Nebuchadnezzar, he would be well over 120 years old at the time of Esther's story. The author(s) may have wanted the reader to understand that long life results from strict adherence to the Mosaic Law and its associated traditions, as is reflected in other literature of the period (e.g., Ecclesiasticus 1:12, 20; 3:6).

Mordecai's dream introduces several apocalyptic elements into the story of Esther. Most prominent is determinism, which reveals that God had already decided what to do (11:12). The rest of the story merely records the outworking of that decision, removing the dramatic tension that is so pronounced in biblical Esther. A second point is the distinction between the Jewish people ("the nation of the righteous"; 11:7) and the Gentiles. God will save His people and eradicate their enemies. It is already decided before the story begins.

In 12:1–5, Mordecai informs on the two eunuchs who plot against the king, setting in motion the events of the book. A crucial difference between biblical Esther and the Additions occurs in 12:5, where the king immediately rewards Mordecai for his loyalty. In contrast, the entire story of biblical Esther hinges on the king *not* rewarding Mordecai (see 6:3).

Like an additional set of "bookends," the edicts in Old Greek Esther record the problem and the solution, respectively, by preserving the king's decrees word for word (the claim of 11:1). (See 13:1–7, Addition B, and 16:1–24, Addition E.)

The prayers of Mordecai and Esther provide a third pair of changes at the very center of the Additions (Addition C, 13:8–14:19, and Addition D, 15:1–16). Mordecai's prayer explains why he refused to bow down to Haman (13:12). Esther's prayer reveals something more.

2 Old Greek *(Esther 14:1–11:1)*

The prayer of Esther, like the prayer of her uncle, reveals a deep disdain for the Gentiles (the "uncircumcised" in 14:15; note 14:18) and links the fate of the Jewish people to the glory of the one true God. Fundamentally, the contest is not between two dragons or two peoples but between the living God and worthless idols. In the end, the king orders his subjects to celebrate the rescue of the Jewish people (16:22–23), and many Gentiles convert to the Jewish faith (8:17).

The author(s) of the Additions changed biblical Esther 6:1 from a description of the king's insomnia to a divine act of intervention ("the Lord removed sleep from the king"). So also Esther's entrance into the throne room and the king's positive response (biblical Esther 5:1–2) is changed to allow a direct act of God for Esther's deliverance (Addition 15:8).

In the end, it's easy to see that the Additions to Esther make three points for the Jewish people living under Greek domination at the end of the third and beginning of the second centuries BC: (1) everything is in God's hands, and its outcome is predetermined; (2) it's official (copies of the royal decrees are included); and (3) God's people, under similar oppression today, can have the same positive outcome as Mordecai and Esther by obeying the Law and keeping the traditions.

3 The Prayer of Manasseh

Old Greek Esther hinges on two prayers, at the heart of the book. Prayer is likewise central to this addition. The starting point for any appeal to God for rescue is His great power. If He cannot help, there's no point in asking. The first thing God reveals about Himself in Scripture is His power, that He created the universe out of nothing. He spoke the Word and the universe burst into being. He continues to hold it together and keep it ordered.

Genesis reveals an all-powerful, righteous, loving God. The Prayer of Manasseh brings all three of these facts together in its invocation (vv. 1–8). Manasseh states that the patriarchs (Abraham, Isaac, and Jacob) did not sin against God (v. 8). This is untrue in a strict sense. But compared to the terrible sins committed by Manasseh, and seen from his perspective, they would certainly appear sinless. We see something of the same sensitivity to past sin in St. Paul, who can describe himself as the "foremost" sinner because he forcibly tried to get Christians to abandon their faith (1 Timothy 1:15; see Acts 26:11). Manasseh, in his prayer, humbles himself before the Lord. Having confessed his sins (vv. 9–10), he "bends[s] the knee of [his] heart."

James offers similar counsel to Christians (James 4:8–10). Although he appeals to God's mercy, he makes no mention of how a righteous God might overlook sin and provide forgiveness. In Romans 3:21–31, Paul shows how God resolves the dilemma of retaining His own righteousness while declaring unrighteous people to be righteous. Only by means of the cross, of Christ crucified for the sins of the world, can a righteous God forgive the sins of people. The only basis Manasseh has for his appeal that God would forgive him is that it would demonstrate God's goodness (v. 13). So Manasseh ends with a promise to praise God for His deliverance (v. 15).

Like Manasseh in this prayer, those enduring foreign subjugation in the Time between the Testaments could point out that destruction of God's people would dishonor God (as Moses pointed out in Exodus 32:9–14) and that forgiving them would show God's goodness (as in this prayer). A promise to praise God often accompanied this appeal, as David prayed in Psalm 51:13–17.

As we bend the knee of our hearts at the foot of the cross, we see the deliverer whom God has provided for our rescue from bondage to sin and domination by Satan—Jesus Christ, the Righteous.

4 The Prayer of Azariah and the Song of the Three Holy Children

We now come to yet another set of prayers and praises to God, the most common form of additions in the Apocrypha. When Nebuchadnezzer deported Azariah, Hananiah, and Mishael from Jerusalem to Babylon in 605 BC, the chief official renamed them Abednego, Shadrach, and Meshach (Daniel 1:7). Like the Jews in Israel in the second century BC, when both of these additions were probably made to Daniel, they faced pressure to abandon their faith and their traditions for the sake of survival. Refusal to assimilate to the dominant Gentile culture put their lives on the line.

An oriental monarch enjoyed the religious as well as political devotion of his subjects. Considered an offspring of the gods, the king solidified the submission of his people through worship of his image. Add to this the human ego and the tendency of power to corrupt a person, and you have Nebuchadnezzar boasting that no god would ever be able to rescue disobedient subjects from his hand (Daniel 3:15).

The response of the three faithful Jews reflects a tremendous trust in the Lord (Daniel 3:16–18). Their faith and obedience does not depend on God's rescue—it leaves that decision to God. Yet the confidence shown by these three contrasts sharply with the confession of sin in the Prayer of Azariah (vv. 1–9). Common in apocryphal works, the confession reflects the conviction that Gentile oppression continues for the same reason it began: Israel's sinful rebellion against the Lord (thus the fall of Jerusalem to the Babylonians in 587 BC). God is always true and right (He really is). But people in the Time between the Testaments assumed that present suffering must flow from past sins, such as what Jesus' disciples concluded about the man born blind in John 9. In this view, the road back to God's favor begins with confession and absolution, which is embodied in the Prayer of Azariah.

This understanding of suffering and its cause fails to take into account God's larger purpose. For example, God may ask an individual to suffer so that someone else may come to faith (such as the man born blind in John 9 or Lazarus's death and resurrection in John 11). The suffering of a nation may be necessary to advance God's plans elsewhere so that the Gospel might go forth into all the world. The proper response when facing hard times is trust in the living God, a trust that figures prominently in the Prayer of Azariah (vv. 11–13). God is faithful and His people can depend on Him to keep His covenant.

Readers who have not lived in war zones where violence has razed cities, killed large portions of the population, caused people to be taken captive to foreign lands, and murdered friends and family for their faith may not appreciate the strength and depth of hostility felt by faithful Jews against the Gentiles. The desire to see God's just retribution upon the Gentiles (Prayer of Azariah vv. 21–22) contrasts sharply with Jesus' outreach and approval of foreigners (see Matthew 8:5–13; 15:21–28). Jesus touched a very raw nerve when He refused to condemn the foreigners who had wrought such suffering on the people living in Israel for so long.

In the addition to Daniel, the Song of the Three Holy Children, God answers Azariah's prayer (vv. 1–22) by sending His angel to cool the flames and save the three men. They respond with a benediction, a song of praise to God that calls all of creation to join with them (vv. 23–68). They lead the chorus (vv. 29–34) and invite the rest of God's works to bless the name of the Lord with them, much like Psalm 148. When God blesses His people, He acts favorably on their behalf, such as the rescue of the three men in the furnace. When God's people bless Him, they praise Him for who He is and for what He has done. The call to praise the Lord begins with the heavens (the first of the works of the Lord, vv. 36–51) and then extends to the earth (vv. 52–59) and finally includes people (vv. 60–66). The sequence roughly follows the order of creation in Genesis 1. The call to human beings to join in the praise of God narrows from all people (v. 60) to Israel (v. 61) to the priests of God (v. 62) and then expands outward to include His servants (v. 63) and all the righteous (vv. 64–65). The three men in the furnace finally call one another to praise the Lord for their rescue (v. 66) and return to focus on God Himself (vv. 67–68). These prayers are beautiful and worthy of our use even today.

5 Bel and the Dragon

Bel, like the Canaanite "baal," is a title meaning "lord." He is Marduk, the chief deity of the region of Babylon, who was given credit for producing the universe (recorded in *Enuma Elish*). The story opens with a challenge to Daniel to prove his beliefs about idols, as when Elijah faced the priests of Baal (1 Kings 18). Such contests put the believer's life on the line.

In the story, Daniel combines a steadfast trust in the living God with godly use of reason. Experience teaches us that inanimate objects (such as idols) do not move, eat, drink, and so forth. Deducing some kind of secret entrance, Daniel has ashes spread on the floor in the presence of the king alone. The secret comes to light the next morning, and the priests and their families pay for their failure with their lives. The wives and the children shared the punishment because they participated in the deception, as did the family of Achan in the Bible (Joshua 7). The original readers of this story are reminded of the folly of idolatry. The Gentiles who oppressed them so severely in the third and second centuries BC worshiped only worthless sticks and stones.

The Dragon is the topic in its own story (vv. 23–30). As is done in a modern game show, the king raises the difficulty level in round two of this theological contrast. The "dragon" may have been an extraordinarily large snake or some other reptilian creature. But unlike Bel, it was certainly alive. Once again, Daniel maintains his loyalty to God (v. 25) and uses his intellect to prove that the beast, although alive, is mortal. The mixture he produces contains three flammable substances: pitch, fat, and hair. Daniel may have concluded that such a mixture would oxidize rapidly in the digestive track of the animal and the expanding gases would kill it. We would need some myth busters to actually try this to determine whether the concoction in the story would actually work as described. The results as recorded were impressive and undeniable (v. 27) but led to Daniel almost becoming a meal himself.

Round three reveals a contest that Daniel is sure to lose, or so it seems (the lions' den; vv. 31–42). His enemies throw him into a den with seven starved lions and leave him there for six days (note the contrasts between this addition and the biblical story in Daniel 6). Daniel's intellect cannot help him now—only direct action by the Lord can rescue him from his situation.

The original readers of these additions to Daniel must have felt as if they also were surrounded by lions in this story. Weaker than the surrounding nations, God's people suffered throughout the third and second centuries BC at the hands of one Gentile nation after another. They found themselves in as hopeless a situation as Daniel, and unable to help themselves.

In this addition to the Book of Daniel, God sends help by means of the prophet Habakkuk, who prophesied in Jerusalem in the years before it fell to Nebuchadnezzer (587 BC). Since this story of Daniel takes place under Cyrus the Great (who ruled Persia, 559–530 BC), it is likely the prophet Habakkuk had finished his course on earth years before. It may be that the author of the addition chose Habakkuk because the prophet struggled with the questions common in the author's day, such as where is God in the midst of all this injustice and suffering? Habakkuk concludes his book (only three chapters long) with a note of patient trust for God to work justice in His own time. Habakkuk 3:17–19 speaks to all God's people who face suffering and want with no clear end in sight: "Yet I will rejoice in the LORD; I will take joy in the God of my salvation. GOD, the Lord, is my strength" (3:18–19a). As Paul will say later, quoting Habakkuk 2:4, "The righteous shall live by faith" (Romans 1:17).

Conclusion

The additions to the apocryphal books are among the most interesting literature from the Time between the Testaments, mostly because they are simply beautiful prayers or examples of excellent storytelling. These stories are also interesting in the way they were used in recent centuries by critics of the Bible.

The critics assumed that the process of adding to books of the Hebrew Old Testament illustrated how most biblical books were actually composed. They assumed that a shorter, simpler document evolved over time to become the books we know today. Unfortunately for critical views, there is no manuscript evidence for what they propose. In fact, there is an opposite example in the story of Jeremiah. Because Hebrew Jeremiah is so repetitive, a scribe from the Time between the Testaments actually edited the book to make it shorter, about 2,700 words shorter. So while we have manuscript evidence that an Old Testament book was made shorter, we have no manuscript evidence to support the critics' claims about an evolution of the Hebrew Old Testament. The inspired Word endures beyond its critics yet again to bless us still today.

Concluding Activities

Conclude the session with an appropriate prayer and distribute the study leaflet for week 6.

Reverence the Divine Laws

2 Maccabees

Preparing for the Session

Central Focus

God's people highly value commitment to the Lord and His teaching—even in the face of persecution. The Lord often works through hardship to deliver His people from evil.

Objectives

That participants, led by the Holy Spirit working through God's Word, will

1. understand the importance of the temple in God's plan of salvation;
2. recognize the importance of suffering in the outworking of God's plan of salvation; and
3. understand that Jesus, by His incarnation, replaces the temple and, by His death, ends the sacrificial system connected to it.

Note for the small-group leaders: Lesson notes and other materials you will need begin on page 65.

For the Lecture Leader

Session Plan

Worship

Begin the session with the hymn printed in the study leaflet. Accompaniments are available in denominational hymnals, such as *Lutheran Service Book* or *Lutheran Worship* (refer to hymnal index). (Note: Concordia Publishing House has available *The Concordia Organist.* All the initial worship hymns in the LifeLight courses are included in this resource. It's especially helpful for mission congregations and small parishes. See the list of study resources on p. 7.) Follow with this prayer:

Prayer

Father, thank You for the tabernacle You gave to Moses and for the temple You built in Jerusalem as a place Your people could come to find You. Thank You for fulfilling the pattern of the temple in Your Son, our Savior, Jesus Christ, and in His sacrifice, which paid for our sins once and for all. Pour out on us Your Holy Spirit so that we, the living stones built on the foundation of Christ Jesus, might share the Gospel and show Christ's love in all the places You have called us to serve. Amen.

Lecture Presentation

Introduction

The writer to the Hebrews declares in the great faith chapter of the Bible, "Some were tortured, refusing to accept release, so that they might rise again to a better life. Others suffered mocking and flogging, and even chains and imprisonment" (11:35–36). He likely has in mind the suffering of believers during the Time between the Testaments, perhaps even Eleazar, the six brothers, and their mother described in 2 Maccabees 6–7.

In the early centuries of the Church, these chapters of 2 Maccabees gave an example to early Christians for passive resistance to persecution and for how to write a martyr story.

In fact, early Christians so closely associated themselves with these martyrs from the Time between the Testaments that their names were added to the list of early Christian martyrs. For these reasons alone, 2 Maccabees is important book for Christians. Let's see what else we can learn from its message.

The Jerusalem temple stands center stage in 2 Maccabees. For the author(s) of 2 Maccabees, the temple and the traditional values of the Jewish culture offered the only path to independence, national security, and economic well-being. Following the general principles laid out in Deuteronomy 28, they believed their obedience to God would lead to blessing, but deviation from His Law would lead to destruction. Although God would preserve His temple (2 Maccabees records three separate threats to it), He would also discipline His wayward people with foreign domination and oppression. Only the blood of the faithful martyrs would turn His anger away from His people, as shown by the book's turning point in 6:18–7:42.

The period covered in 2 Maccabees is from 185 to 160 BC. During this time, several Seleucid rulers exercised power, including Antiochus III (222–187 BC), Seleucus IV (187–175 BC), and Antiochus IV Epiphanes (175–164 BC). The Jerusalem temple suffered pillaging and desecration during the reign of each of these rulers, the worst of which was Antiochus IV Epiphanes, who is often considered the fulfillment of the "little horn" prophecy in Daniel 7–8. He was a precursor to the infamous "man of lawlessness" in 2 Thessalonians 2, the ultimate Antichrist of the end times. The desecration of the Jerusalem temple by Antiochus IV Epiphanes, the rebellion by the Maccabees, and the rededication of the temple are remembered in the Jewish festival Hanukkah. The opening letters of 2 Maccabees ask the Jewish community in Egypt to keep this festival, serving as an introduction to the book.

1 The Two Letters *(2 Maccabees 1:1–2:18)*

When the Ptolemies ruled Israel, political concerns would not have hindered communication between the Jewish colony in Egypt and the Jews in Judea. Relations between the two groups may have been relatively positive up to the point that the Seleucids conquered Israel. The author of the first letter in 2 Maccabees (1:1–9) writes to the Egyptian Jews to encourage them to observe Hanukkah, the festival of lights celebrating the rededication of the temple after its desecration by Antiochus IV Epiphanes (described in ch. 5). By observing Hanukkah, a semblance of Jewish unity would be maintained and the priority and importance of the Jerusalem temple would be affirmed (see also Tobit 1:3–4).

The second letter (2 Maccabees 1:10–2:18) looks back to Jeremiah, who was active until the fall of Jerusalem in 587 BC, and Nehemiah, who led the rebuilding of the temple and the city after the return of the exiles (445 BC). Combustion of the naptha (1:30–36) and preservation of the temple furniture (2:4–5) show God's approval of the rebuilt temple and the connection it had with the first temple built by Solomon (960 BC). The author's point would be that the second temple, though poor and plain in appearance compared to the beautiful temple of Solomon, was every bit as important and deserved the loyalty and support of all Jewish people, including those in Egypt.

2 The First Threat *(2 Maccabees 2:19–3:40)*

The much larger historical work of Jason of Cyrene is summarized in this section of 2 Maccabees. Like a condensation from *Reader's Digest*, the goal was to make the work easier to read and memorable. Cyrene, a city in modern Libya (Africa), was known as the "Athens of Africa" in the third century BC; it was home to a well-reputed school of philosophy. "Jason of Cyrene" is otherwise unknown except for this reference. The authors of this summary want to tell the story of Hanukkah and the Maccabean wars, no doubt to encourage readers to stand fast in their faith against the pressures they faced. As currently illustrated in the story of the Maccabees, when they are faithful to God, He intervenes to save them from their enemies.

The story opens during the high priesthood of Onias III (198–174 BC). The story told in 2 Maccabees often seems melodramatic, depicting the "good guys" as almost saintly in their virtue and the "bad guys" as thoroughly evil. Whether this was the work of the original author (Jason) or the editors is unknown. At the direction of King Seleucus IV (reigned 187–175 BC), Heliodorus leads the first attack on the temple (3:1–4:6). In response to the entreaties of Onias and the people of Jerusalem, a glorious rider wearing a magnificent decorative covering attacks Heliodorus and renders him senseless.

Modern readers should remember that the editors envisioned their work being read or recounted by memory to groups of people. The exaggerated "goodness" and "badness" of the characters was designed to entertain as well as educate and encourage. Our own culture has used the same device (melodrama) for similar purposes. Those familiar with the "Dudley Do-Right" sagas, with "Snidely Whiplash" as the villain and "Nell Fenwick" as the damsel in distress, will remember that the stories always ended with a positive moral communicated in a way that captured the attention of the audience. The editors (and possibly the author) of 2 Maccabees do something similar when they paint their verbal pictures with broad strokes of virtue and villainy. The difference, of course, is that real people are suffering and dying in the history of the Maccabees.

Initially, the prayer by Onias for the stricken Heliodorus (3:31–34) looks like a reflection of Jesus' command to His followers in Matthew 5:43–44, "Love your enemies and pray for those who persecute you." A careful reading of the text, however, reveals that Onias prays for

Heliodorus due to fear of reprisal from Seleucus IV (3:32). In contrast, Jesus challenges His followers to operate out of genuine concern for the welfare of others—including enemies—and not out of self-interest. The editors of 2 Maccabees spell out the moral of the story about the first attack on the temple in 3:38–40. Heaven is watching. Readers of the New Testament might recognize a similar point in Jesus' parable of the tenets (Matthew 21:33–46).

3 The Second Threat *(2 Maccabees 4:1–6:17)*

This section begins by introducing Antiochus IV Epiphanes (4:7; ruled 175–164 BC). Just as this work introduced the term "Judaism" (2:21) to refer to the traditional faith and lifestyle of God's people under the Mosaic Law, so it also introduces the term "hellenization" (4:13) to describe how the Seleucids changed their cultural values and religious beliefs to accommodate the Greeks. This process continued long after the death of Alexander the Great in 323 BC. Ironically, the villainous Greek language of the Time between the Testaments becomes what God's new heroes in the New Testament speak as they go everywhere, proclaiming Jesus in this common tongue and eventually witnessing the conversion of Alexander's homeland to Christianity.

However, back in Jerusalem, the wickedness and apostasy of the high priests described in 4:1–5:10 set the stage for God's judgment, as recorded in 5:11 and following. Ambition motivated several men to vie for the high priesthood, and corruption made it possible. Jason (Onias's brother) bribes his way into office under Antiochus IV Epiphanes (4:7–9). Menelaus (brother of Onias's enemy Simon; 3:4–5) later out-bribes him and takes over (4:23–24). His occupancy of the office of high priest created problems because he was not from the high priestly family. Perhaps the best analogy today comes from Great Britain. Imagine the outcry if a commoner bribed some reigning foreign overlord to be named king! Suddenly all the inheritance-based relationships that endured for centuries would lose their reason for existing. The entire social and political system was in danger of coming unglued. The stories of such intrigue roll on and on throughout the book.

But alongside of this, the author explains the purpose of the suffering that God permitted His people to experience (6:12–17). This is discipline from God. This explanation reflects Deuteronomy 8:5 and is also reflected in the New Testament by Paul (1 Corinthians 11:32) and the author of Hebrews (Hebrews 12:5–6, citing Proverbs 3:11–12). Even construction accidents should warn people to turn from evil and back to the Lord (Luke 13:1–5).

4 The Turning Point *(2 Maccabees 6:18–13:26)*

As noted at the beginning of our lecture, the martyrdom of Eleazar, the seven brothers, and their mother will turn back God's wrath and spur His compassion. Martyrdom accomplishes several things in 2 Maccabees. Later, even New Testament authors would affirm the role and value of suffering for the faith (Acts 5:41; 2 Corinthians 4:17). However, only the ultimate martyr, Jesus Christ, can truly turn back the wrath of God against sinners.

Now God raises up His champion, introduced in 2 Maccabees 5:27 as the leader of a small group of faithful believers—Judas Maccabeus takes center stage in the story of Hanukkah (ch. 8). The author confirms the turning point has been reached in 8:5, "for the wrath of the Lord had turned to mercy."

With the help of God ("El-eazer" means "God's help"; 8:23), Judas and his brothers defeat the superior forces of Nicanor. In chapter 8, the author passes up the opportunity to describe the strategy or tactics of the Maccabean army but describes several aspects of their piety: prayer, Scripture reading, Sabbath observance, and support for widows and orphans. Their victory flows from their devotion to the Lord, to the temple, and to the Mosaic Law (8:36).

The end of Antiochus IV Epiphanes (ch. 9) climaxes in the purification of the temple (10:1–9). On the anniversary of its desecration, the sanctuary was purified and religious activities resumed in conformity to the Mosaic Law. (Comparing 1 Maccabees 1:54 to 1 Maccabees 4:52 reveals a three-year time span between the desecration and the purification.) Those who cleansed the temple decreed an annual observance of this victory for all Jewish people. The author explains the eight-day length of the celebration by noting that the Maccabees could not celebrate the Feast of Booths or Tabernacles, which had been held a few weeks earlier when they were in hiding (see Leviticus 23:33–43). They transposed the length of that festival to Hanukkah. The Hanukkah legend of the one-day supply of oil for the lampstands lasting all eight days comes from later Jewish tradition.

5 The Third Threat and Epilogue *(2 Maccabees 10:10–15:39)*

In true melodramatic form, the author describes the victories of the Maccabees over their enemies (10:10–38). He includes a description of an angelic appearance that demonstrates God's intervention on their behalf (10:29–31). Any Jewish audience listening to a reading or an oration of this part of the story would have no doubt stood up and cheered the valiant Maccabees as they cut down the despised Gentiles who had made life so miserable for the Jewish people.

The same divine aid in the form of an angel defeats Lysias (11:1–12) and leads him to conclude that the Jewish forces cannot be defeated. The letters of 11:16–38 provide an official "seal" to the outcome of the battle as well as reintroduce a relatively new force in Israel's politics (mentioned in 4:11)—the Romans.

A key element in the next story is Judas Maccabeus's trust in the Lord and tactical boldness (2 Maccabees 13:9–17). Readers familiar with Judges may see a parallel between Gideon's successful surprise attack on a superior force (Judges 7) and that of Judas in this chapter.

The storyteller concludes his tale of God's protection of the temple by recounting the reception of a golden sword from God (15:17) and the prayer of Judas Maccabeus (15:22–26). The end of Nicanor may sound gruesome to modern ears but reflects God's justice and Middle Eastern sensibilities (as is still the case today). Imagine an oral presentation of 2 Maccabees (whether by reading or by memory); the last few verses of the book make a great "sign-off."

Conclusion

It may be hard for Christians to see why the temple was so important for God's people in the centuries before the earthly ministry of Jesus. Perhaps the best way to think of the temple is to view it as heaven's embassy on earth. Just as a foreign embassy's grounds become foreign soil by national agreement, so the temple could be viewed as a bit of heaven on earth. The "ambassador's seat," the ark of the covenant, was the "heart" of the temple. The temple and the sacrificial system highlighted the gulf between God and man created by sin.

A connection between the sacrifice of animals under the Mosaic Law and the sacrifice of martyrs during the period of the Maccabees is seen in the Book of 2 Maccabees. Life is the blood (Genesis 9:4–5). A "blood sacrifice" paid the Law's penalty of sin and silenced the Law (see Leviticus 16:11–19). Since no animal could fully atone for the sin of humanity, the whole Mosaic sacrificial system could only remind people of the problem and point to a future solution. Jesus provided that solution on the cross. As God Incarnate, He made the final and effective sacrifice for all sin (Galatians 3:13–14; 2 Corinthians 5:21; Hebrews 9:11–10:18). Not only does Jesus replace the temple as the place where the fullness of God dwells bodily (Colossians 2:9), but He also brings an end to the sacrifices connected to the temple with the cross.

The author of 2 Maccabees misunderstands the purpose of martyrdom when he sees the death of God's faithful people as the agent for changing God's wrath to kindness (2 Maccabees 7:37–38; 8:5). God does not assign to someone else the terrible suffering and death necessary to turn His heart from wrath to mercy. Instead, He takes the job on Himself. He becomes a human being (thus, born under the Law) to redeem those under the Law (Galatians 4:4–5). In Christ, He pays the price of atonement Himself (Romans 3:21–26).

Martyrdom does play a significant role in God's work in the world. It highlights the hostility of the devil, the world, and sinful human nature toward God and His people (as with John the Baptist; Matthew 11:12). It also provides a witness to the world (for the word *martyr* comes from the Greek word for "witness"). As the church father Tertullian would later write of the martyrs, "The blood of Christians is seed" (*Apology*, ch. 50). Even today, Christians suffer and die for the sake of the Gospel as witnesses to the truth—Jesus Christ, the ultimate witness (Revelation 1:5; 3:14).

Concluding Activities

Conclude the session with an appropriate prayer and distribute the study leaflet for week 7.

Strength Comes from Heaven

1 Maccabees

Preparing for the Session

Central Focus

Like Phinehas in Numbers 25, the Maccabees show such zeal for the name of the Lord in the face of Gentile opposition that God's wrath against His people ceases and they resecure for themselves the priesthood.

Objectives

That participants, led by the Holy Spirit working through God's Word, will

1. see the Lord is at work in history to accomplish His goal, the salvation of souls;
2. understand the nature of the "abomination of desolation" and its connection to the end times; and
3. appreciate the connection between the period of the Maccabees and the ministry of Jesus.

Note for the small-group leaders: Lesson notes and other materials you will need begin on page 67.

For the Lecture Leader

Session Plan

Worship

Begin the session with the hymn printed in the study leaflet. Accompaniments are available in denominational hymnals, such as *Lutheran Service Book* or *Lutheran Worship* (refer to hymnal index). (Note: Concordia Publishing House has available *The Concordia Organist*. All the initial worship hymns in the LifeLight courses are included in this resource. It's especially helpful for mission congregations and small parishes. See the list of study resources on p. 7.) Follow with this prayer:

Prayer

Father, thank You for sending Your Son, Jesus Christ, to save us. Thank You for Your Holy Spirit, who brings us to new life in our Baptism and leads us in faith daily. Fill us with true zeal for You so that we boldly proclaim Your Gospel and follow in the footsteps of our Savior. Grant us wisdom to know Your will and courage and strength to do all to Your glory. In Jesus' holy name. Amen.

Lecture Presentation

Introduction

Whether they cheer for George Washington or Che Guevara, people love freedom fighters. The stories of these people impress and embolden us like few others. 1 Maccabees is just such a story, in which a beleaguered and outnumbered people rises up through hard-won victories to gain their freedom from oppressive foreign rule.

Modeling his story after the historical accounts of Samuel and Kings, the author of 1 Maccabees tells of how the Maccabean family came to occupy the priesthood of Israel. Also like the author(s) of Samuel and Kings in Scripture, the author of 1 Maccabees evaluates each of the people in the story. As they are measured against his own faith-system and the conviction that the Maccabean family alone has divine approval to rule Israel, the historical figures in 1 Maccabees receive a stamp of approval or disapproval.

In the first nine verses, the author turns back the clock by over a century and a half. He recounts very briefly the origin of the present troubles faced by God's people in Israel: Alexander the Great. Before Alexander's conquest of the Mediterranean region, life for the Jewish people under Persian rule (538–330 BC) had been relatively peaceful. After Alexander died (323 BC), control of Israel fell to Ptolemy, son of Lagus, and his heirs. Relations between Ptolemy and the Jewish people got off to a rocky start (some 100,000 people were forcibly relocated to Egypt). Before long, however, things settled down and the Jewish people were permitted to practice their faith and rule themselves as long as they paid their taxes and behaved.

This changed in the early second century BC. The Seleucids had come into possession of Israel, thanks to the able leadership of Antiochus III the Great. Initially, God's people fared relatively well. However, after Antiochus III lost the battle of Smyrna against the Romans (190 BC), conditions grew rapidly worse.

Forced to pay a very large debt, Antiochus III plundered the temples in his domain to get the money, since temples served as ancient banks. Not only did this deeply offend the Jewish people, but it also led to lasting conflict.

However, through the line of divinely approved high priests, God would continue to rule His people. If 2 Maccabees is designed to be recited to an audience as a broad melodrama reinforcing the importance of the temple and Jewish piety, then by contrast, 1 Maccabees presents itself as an objective history, seen through the lenses of Maccabean divine appointment.

1 Antiochus IV Epiphanes and Mattathias *(1 Maccabees 1:10–2:70)*

The chief antagonist to the Jewish people is introduced to us in 1 Maccabees 1:10, Antiochus IV Epiphanes (ruled 175–164 BC). In 1:10–64, the author describes the desecration of the temple, the persecution of the faithful, and the apostasy of many in Jerusalem and Judea. The "abomination of desolation" (literally, "the offensive smell that drives everyone away") finds fulfillment in the unlawful sacrifices offered at the temple to false gods (Daniel 11:31; cf. Matthew 24:15). For a graphic description of the persecutions against the faithful, recall 2 Maccabees, which we studied in the last session.

The writer uses poetical sections and laments to express his deep feelings about the situation. The first of these laments (1:24b–28) occurs immediately following the stripping of the temple by Antiochus IV Epiphanes in 167 BC. Modern readers may not appreciate the depth of feeling that pious Jews had regarding the temple. Because it was not only a national symbol but also a focal point of their faith, it meant more to them than the Eiffel tower to Parisians or Big Ben to Londoners or the National September 11 Memorial to Americans. Even allowing for some exaggeration, the Jerusalem temple and its sacrificial system served as a marker of God's covenant commitment to them, their identity as God's chosen people, and the one place where God and man could meet together (see the Day of Atonement, Leviticus 16).

The protagonists of the story, the family of Mattathias Maccabeus, appear in 2:1–5. The author establishes Mattathias's priestly pedigree by noting his descent from Joarib (Jehoiarib), a descendent of Aaron (see 1 Chronicles 24:1–7). A high priest had to come from such a priestly family. Mattathias and his family have moved to Modein (a mountainous area about twenty miles northwest of Jerusalem) to escape the deteriorating situation in Jerusalem (see 2 Maccabees 5:27). But the trouble follows them to their new home.

Mattathias's lament of grief in 2:7–13 is reminiscent of the emotions associated with the fall of Jerusalem and the destruction of the temple by the Babylonians in 586 BC, which was described in the biblical Book of Lamentations. The depth of feeling he expresses is echoed two centuries later in the anger felt toward Stephen, the first Christian martyr, when he was accused of speaking against the temple and the Mosaic Law (see Acts 6:13–14). With the incarnation, the temple becomes obsolete; with the cross, the animal sacrifices serve no purpose. In the second century BC, however, the temple and its sacrifices still served as the point of contact between God and His people as well as the singular identity marker of the Jewish nation.

Mattathias reacts to the apostasy of an unnamed Jew who came forward to offer pagan sacrifice in Modein (2:15–26). Like Phinehas, whose zeal for the Lord resulted in his appointment as priest (Numbers 25), Mattathias ignites a revolution by killing the Jewish man and the Gentile officer.

The theme of retribution dominates 2:42–70. In contrast to Jesus' admonition to "love your enemies" (Matthew 5:43–44), Mattathias directs his sons to "pay back the Gentiles in full" (2:68a). The fact that Jesus refused to condemn "sinners" immediately, but conversed openly with them, angered many of His contemporaries. This explains the rejection He experienced at His hometown of Nazareth (Luke 4:16–30).

2 Judas Maccabeus, part 1 *(1 Maccabees 3:1–5:68)*

Just as Mattathias's lament preceded the story of his act of defiance at Modein, so a song of praise introduces Judas's victorious campaign. (For a similar song celebrating the victory of God's people, see the Song of Moses in Exodus 15.) Judas affirms that "strength comes from heaven" (that is, from God; 3:19b), but he also uses his skill and advantage for ambush, which the terrain provides against Seron's army. The combination of complete dependence upon God and the use of all human abilities and resources also appears in other apocryphal work, particularly Judith. The temple once more appears as a central concern to the author and, if accurately portraying Judas and his followers, the combatants (3:43).

The key to success for Judas and his band is the Lord. The fighters employ prayer and fasting as well as consulting the Scriptures before engaging the enemy in battle (3:46–48). The story of Gideon (Judges 7) may have motivated the release of those soldiers who were distracted or afraid (3:56). In the end, they recognize that it is up to God (3:60). Their victory over Gorgias (4:1–25) proves the power of God over the Gentiles and their idols (4:11), a theme apparent in the ten plagues of the exodus as well (Exodus 9:14).

As Goliath fell to David (1 Samuel 17), so Gorgias's replacement, Lysias, falls to Judas (4:26–35). Following their victory, the Israelites return to Jerusalem and inspect the temple. Three years had passed since Antiochus IV Epiphanes had desecrated it, and its priests had fled, abandoning it to neglect. Cleaned up, and with new altar and appointments, the temple was dedicated and the people celebrated for eight days, the length of the Feast of Booths that had occurred a few weeks earlier (4:36–59). So the feast of Hanukkah is born.

Hostility toward the Jewish people, especially in the face of a resurgent Jewish state, moved some of the Gentiles to plot the destruction of the Jewish populations in their areas (1 Maccabees 5:9–23). Splitting his forces into several effective raiding parties, Judas rescues the Jewish populations under threat and returns them to Judea. He achieves success against Timothy, an enemy commander, by attacking from behind with a great deal of noise, which unsettles the nerves of their opponents in (5:24–44).

The incident recorded in 5:55–63 proves that the Hasmonean dynasty (descendants of Mattathias and his sons) alone have divine approval. The author makes his point clear in 5:62: God gives deliverance only through one family. The priests who die in 5:65–68 stepped outside of their priestly role, and so they die as combatants. The word "unwisely" in 5:67 denotes a lack of counsel, an action taken without proper consideration. God has appointed the Maccabees to lead.

3 Judas Maccabeus, part 2 *(1 Maccabees 6:1–9:22)*

The initial great success of Judas, it seems, cannot last. He remains the greatest hero of the Maccabean dynasty, but the writer shows him to be a flesh-and-blood man struggling to hold on to the victories God has given him.

Antiochus IV Epiphanes built the citadel (or Acra, from the Greek "acropolis," meaning "high place") after he sacked the temple and defiled it with unlawful sacrifices. It was a compound surrounded by formidable walls and populated by Gentiles and pro-Greek Jews. Attacking it was tantamount to attacking the Seleucids themselves. Gentile forces begin the first of several new incursions into Israel (6:18–33). So the attack by Jewish forces on the citadel near the temple in 162 BC prompted the new king to act.

A considerable force marches on Jerusalem from the south; Beth-zechariah lies about eleven miles south of Jerusalem. The reference to the juice of grapes and mulberries (6:34) may reflect the practice of giving war elephants wine to drink (mentioned by at least one ancient naturalist). How did this work? If the elephants regularly consumed wine and developed a fondness for it, then showing them wine would get them excited and move them in the direction of the wine. The Gentiles are drawing on every device available to them in their lust for reconquest. The Jewish forces fight bravely, epitomized by the death of Maccabean brother Eleazar Avaran as he was trying to kill an enemy war elephant (6:43–46). Nevertheless, they lose the battle and seek refuge in the temple compound (6:48–54). Both the Gentiles and the Jewish armies experience the setbacks. But a change in the high priesthood proves devastating to Judas.

Alcimus, a descendant from Moses' brother Aaron, was qualified to serve as a priest, and so the gullible law experts (the "scribes"; 7:12) lay down their arms when the enemy commander Bacchides enters Jerusalem. The loss of these Hasideans (see 2:42) weakens Judas's army to the point that the best he can do is to harass the Seleucids and pro-Greek Jews from the countryside (7:21–25).

Nicanor presents yet another threat to the temple (9:26–38). Failing to capture Judas by deceit and treachery, he tries to intimidate the population of Jerusalem by threatening the heart of their nation: God's house (see 1 Kings 8–9). The call for retribution against Nicanor, like all deprecatory psalms, needs to be read in the light of great pain and suffering and an appeal to God's righteousness. It is easy for those who have not suffered to criticize those who have suffered and consequently look for a way to express their sorrow and anger. Like Alcimus, Nicanor dies before he can fulfill his threat (7:39–50).

Judas now sends emissaries to forge an alliance with Rome. Nonaggression, mutual defense, and provisions for changing the details of the treaty compose the agreement (ch. 8). This opened the door for Roman involvement, which would expand greatly in 63 BC. Judas himself falls in battle in 160 BC (9:11–22). In an irony of history, Judas the hero has invited to Jerusalem the people who would not just defile the temple but permanently destroy it. They would likewise destroy the temple of a young preacher from Nazareth by hanging Him upon a cross. But the temple of His body would not stay down; it would rise to reign even over Rome itself. Isn't history remarkable?

4 Jonathan Maccabeus *(1 Maccabees 9:23–12:53)*

In 9:23–31, Jonathan (ruled 160–143 BC) succeeds his brother as leader of the faithful Jewish forces in Israel, elected by the "friends" of Judas. He gathers an apparently small band of the faithful and begins operations, evading Bacchides, who attempts to trap him on the Sabbath (9:43–49). After the death of Alcimus, Bacchides returned to the king and the land had a short respite from war (9:57).

Nevertheless, the pro-Greek faction of the Jews convinces Bacchides to return after that short break (9:58–73). Unable to defeat Jonathan, Bacchides packs up and heads for home. Before he gets very far, Jonathan displays a talent for diplomacy that will serve him and his countrymen very well in the future. He negotiates a peace treaty with Bacchides that not only permits Jews the freedom to practice their religion but also reclaims the captives Bacchides had taken earlier.

Five years of relative peace pass between the end of chapter 9 and the beginning of chapter 10. Yet another struggle for the Seleucid kingship begins when Alexander Epiphanes (or Balas) makes his move in 152 BC. Both he and his rival, Demetrius I, vie for Jewish support, since the Jews occupy the land south of Syria.

Distrusting Demetrius, Jonathan allies his people with Alexander Balas. By accepting Alexander's offer, Jonathan becomes both high priest and king. By skillful diplomacy, Jonathan strengthens his own position and that of his people. Jonathan receives a promotion from "friend" of the king to "chief friend" of the king (10:65).

Jonathan moves up the ladder of success to become one of the "kinsmen of kings" when he defeats the representative of another challenger to the Seleucid throne, Demetrius II Nicator (10:67–89). The events of this period often read like a soap opera as, in one case (11:8–18), a father takes his daughter away from her husband (his son-in-law) and gives her to another man. The son-in-law soon meets his end after losing a battle against the father-in-law, but the father-in-law dies a couple of days later anyway. Whether the son-in-law was to blame for the falling out (per Josephus) or it was the father-in-law (per 1 Maccabees) is impossible to determine.

The author also records Jonathan's military exploits in 11:60–74, where he seems indistinguishable from the Gentile military leaders. Jonathan's diplomatic skills are again highlighted in 12:1–23, where he strengthens bonds with Rome and Sparta. Christians will appreciate the references to the "holy books" (12:9) and God's help (12:15). Finally, Jonathan's instincts fail him in 12:39–53 as his former ally turns on him, capturing him and killing his bodyguard.

5 Simon Maccabeus *(1 Maccabees 13–16)*

The youngest of the Maccabean brothers, Simon, assumes leadership of God's people in 13:1–11 (ruled 142–134 BC). Simon buries Jonathan and his other family members in Modein, where their story began. He erects a monument for them, displaying their armor in the same way Greeks honored their dead, which shows the degree that Greek culture influenced the practices of the faithful. God's people live in the world and thus inevitably reflect the values of their earthly society to some extent.

Under Simon's leadership, Israel finally finds itself released from "the yoke of the Gentiles" (13:41) in 142 BC. With the two contenders for the Seleucid throne fighting each other (Trypho and Demetius II), Simon makes his move. The Acra citadel falls in 141 BC and is purified (13:49–53), the pro-Greek thorn finally removed from the side of God's people in Jerusalem. Free at last, Israel begin a new system of dating based on Simon's rule. Already the head of the government, Simon becomes high priest as well within just a few years (14:47).

Just as Jonathan had died as a result of treachery, so also Simon and two of his sons die at the hands of someone they trusted: Simon's son-in-law (16:11–17). Power passes to Simon's remaining son, John Hyrcanus. Consistent with the theme of the book—that the Hasmoneans are the only legitimate high priestly family—the author ends on the note of John Hyrcanus's ascension to the office of high priest and leader of God's people (16:24).

Conclusion

Four elements of 1 Maccabees may stand out for the modern reader. First, by placing His people in Canaan, God put them in the middle of a great highway. Anyone going from Europe or Asia to Africa (or vice versa) by land would travel through Israel. This would provide them with a regular opportunity to witness as Gentiles noticed how different they were. It would also challenge them to remain faithful in the face of temptation (idolatry) and trial (persecution).

Second, the many names in 1 Maccabees can be very confusing. Dynastic names sound very similar and can only be differentiated by Roman numerals or nicknames. Like readers of the Bible who give up reading in the early chapters of Genesis because of the many unfamiliar names, readers of 1 and 2 Maccabees can become so frustrated that they just give up. I hope you make it to the end.

Third, we need the story of the Maccabees! They fought for religious freedom. They fought for orthodoxy as they understood it, and in these ways they set examples for us. They also shaped the messianic expectations of later generations, which helps us understand the New Testament. The zeal of the Maccabees helps explain the hostile reaction so many of their descendants displayed against Jesus, friend of sinners.

Finally, the actions of Antiochus IV Epiphanes, Daniel's "abomination of desolation," prefigures the period immediately prior to the coming final judgment. The rise of "the man of lawlessness" (2 Thessalonians 2:3–12) and the intense persecution that will occur at that time (Matthew 24:15–35) fulfill the pattern of self-deification, blasphemy, and suffering of God's people recorded in 1 and 2 Maccabees. As you consider their stories, do so with prayer that the Lord would grant you an unshakable faith and endurance that lasts until the end. Through it all, see the faithfulness of the Lord, who preserved His people through innumerable obstacles. Whatever or whoever opposes your faith today, know that your Lord is indomitable. Maranatha! Come, Lord Jesus.

Concluding Activities

Conclude the session with an appropriate prayer and distribute the study leaflet for week 8.

The Lord Foiled Them by the Hand of a Woman

Judith

Preparing for the Session

Central Focus

Even the weakest person, armed with faith and strict adherence to the laws of Moses and the traditions of the elders, can defeat the most powerful Gentile enemies. Trust in God trumps armies of enemies.

Objectives

That participants, led by the Holy Spirit working through God's Word, will

1. remember that the One who dwells within them is stronger than the one who dwells in the world (1 John 4:4);
2. turn to the Lord for help and direction when faced with seemingly overwhelming problems; and
3. appreciate the resources given to them by God to do the work He gives them to do.

Note for the small-group leaders: Lesson notes and other materials you will need begin on page 69.

For the Lecture Leader

Session Plan

Worship

Begin the session with the hymn printed in the study leaflet. Accompaniments are available in denominational hymnals, such as *Lutheran Service Book* or *Lutheran Worship* (refer to hymnal index). (Note: Concordia Publishing House has available *The Concordia Organist*. All the initial worship hymns in the LifeLight courses are included in this resource. It's especially helpful for mission congregations and small parishes. See the list of study resources on p. 7.) Follow with this prayer:

Prayer

Father, guide us by Your Holy Spirit as we face the challenges that confront us every day. Anchor us in Jesus Christ, and instruct us by Your Word so that we stand in faith no matter what the circumstance. Keep us faithful to You, protected from every temptation and strengthened in every trial by Your promise and presence. Remind us that You are always faithful, providing a way through or around every obstacle (1 Corinthians 10:13). Amen.

Lecture Presentation

Introduction (Judith 1:1–10)

Judith is not your average feminist. Medieval and Renaissance painters loved to portrayal her with a sword in one hand and the head of Holofernes in the other. She is a *femme fatale*, "a dangerous woman," who is likewise modest and pious.

Armed with an unshakable faith in the Lord and a keen mind, Judith wins the day when the rest of her village is ready to give up on God. In the tradition of great women in the Hebrew Scriptures, like Jael in Judges 4–5 or Esther in the book named for her, Judith acts as a superheroine who risks her life to defeat those who would harm God's people.

As we have seen, early in the second century BC, the people of God in Israel faced intense pressure to adopt Greek culture, Greek values, and Greek religion. Faithful adherence to the Mosaic Law and the piety of the elders resulted in torture and death. Even after the Maccabean Revolt and the creation of a Jewish state, armed conflict with non-Jews continued. The presence of pro-Greek Jews made the situation ever more complex.

For those fighting for the Jewish side (Torah, temple, and traditions), it must have been hard to "keep the faith." The overwhelming numerical supremacy of the enemy, the number of turncoat neighbors, the difficulty of keeping the alliance between the *Chasidim* and the Hasmoneans, as well as the never-ending political intrigue within the ruling families could easily lead God's people to give up. They needed a hero, someone who embodied the faith and overcame both the strength of the enemy and the weakness of the people. The author of Judith gives them that hero.

The story opens in 593 BC, the twelfth year of Nebuchadnezzar. The author of Judith quickly alerts his readers to the nonhistorical nature of his book by making Nebuchadnezzar an Assyrian ruler. The Assyrians had captured the northern ten tribes (called "Israel" or "Ephraim") by 721 BC. The Babylonians defeated the southern tribes (called "Judah") in 587 BC and led a large number of people into exile. By combining these two historical enemies of God's people, the author of Judith sets the stage for a "super-villain" to appear. The small Jewish nation, humanly speaking, has absolutely no hope of standing firm against Nebuchadnezzar's military machine. God's people in the second century BC must have felt the same way when considering the vast military might of the Gentiles who threatened them.

1 The Enemy *(Judith 2:1–3:10)*

Similar to Sherman's "march to the sea" in the fall of 1864, Holofernes practiced "total war." His scorched-earth tactics demoralized his remaining enemies and brought an earlier end to their resistance. The author's geographical references remind the reader that none of this is historical. For example, the distance between Nineveh and Bectileth near Upper Cilicia (300 miles) is said to have been covered by Holofernes's army in three days, which is clearly impossible. Holofernes and his army constitute an unstoppable force, rolling over one country after another with hardly a speed bump to slow them down. How can Judah, small and weak, stand against such military might?

Any hope they had that Holofernes might be slowed or stopped by the city-states along the coast on the route he would take to reach Judah evaporated as those cities surrender without a fight (2:28–3:10). The situation actually gets worse for those in Judea as Holofernes augments his army with the best soldiers from the city-states that surrender (2:6).

Then Holofernes makes an offer: he will leave the people and the land alone in exchange for exclusive worship of Nebuchadnezzar. This makes sense from the perspective of an oriental ruler, since it unites political and religious control of the people under his rule. However, it denies the true God and destroys the relationship He established with His people (the First Commandment; Exodus 20:3 and Deuteronomy 5:7). Old Testament readers will remember the three young men and the fiery furnace (Daniel 3) as well as Daniel in the lions' den (Daniel 6). New Testament readers will recall Satan's temptation of Christ, offering the glory and power of the world's kingdom in exchange for worship and submission to him (Matthew 4:9–10; Luke 4:7–8). God's people have regularly faced First Commandment challenges throughout history and still do today.

2 Judah Prepares *(Judith 4)*

By mentioning the temple in 4:1–7, the author reflects the same values as 1 and 2 Maccabees. The cleansing mentioned in Judith 4:3 looks back at the purification done by the exiles (end of the sixth century BC) through the lens of the recent cleansing performed by the Maccabees (164 BC). The people of God who suffered in the second century BC looked back at the history of their ancestors to answer the question "why me?" or "why us?" Disobedience to the Law and neglect of the traditions had, it was thought, led to the destruction of Jerusalem in 587 BC and domination by Gentiles. By applying that model to their own situation, they concluded that neglect of the temple and the Law of Moses had led to their present suffering at the hand of foreigners.

It may seem strange to people familiar with the Hebrew Scriptures to read that the high priest coordinated the defense of Judea (Judith 4:6–7). In the absence of a king (the monarchy ended in the early sixth century BC) or a governor (such as was the case under Persian rule), the high priest assumed the power of a secular ruler. This was particularly true in the last half of the second century BC. Something of this power can still be seen in the legal proceedings against Jesus in the New Testament. Pontius Pilate governed the Roman province of Judea-Samaria, but the high priest exercised power within limits set by Rome. Jesus stood before him prior to appearing in Pilate's court (Mark 14:53–65; John 18:12–14, 19–24).

Dothan (Judith 4:6) lies about forty miles north of Jerusalem. The individual villages of Bethulia and Betomesthaim are likely inventions of the author. In this story, the only approach to Jerusalem lies over a narrow pass near these villages. Although the author of Judith draws heavily from the Hebrew Scriptures and from Middle Eastern history to create his characters, this detail may well owe its origin to the Battle of Thermopylae in 480 BC, when King Leonidas of Sparta faced the superior Persian army. The author's geographical invention sets the stage for Judith's act of faith to provide rescue not only for her village but for the temple in Jerusalem as well, if only the people will humble themselves and believe.

Readers of the New Testament will recognize the basic principle illustrated by Judith 4:8–15. Peter advises, "Humble yourselves, therefore, under the mighty hand of God so that at the proper time He may exalt you, casting all your anxieties on Him, because He cares for you" (1 Peter 5:6–7). The author of Judith emphasizes the rituals associated with repentance and sorrow (sackcloth, ashes, fasting, and prayer), whereas Peter focuses on the spiritual act of self-denial and submission to God's will.

3 The Die Is Cast *(Judith 5–7)*

Holofernes and his generals make the same mistake that Goliath made in 1 Samuel 17:42. They judge God's people by their outward appearance (Judith 5:23). God often chose the "least of all" for His purpose in Scripture. Gideon described himself as the least important member of his family, which was the smallest clan in his tribe (Judges 6:15). Even King Saul recognized his lack of qualifications for the job of Israel's leader, since he came from the poorest family in the smallest tribe of Israel (1 Samuel 9:21). It was not the first time that an enemy general underestimated the power of the living God when assessing the potential military power of His people. The supreme commander of the Assyrian army made exactly the same mistake when besieging Jerusalem in 701 BC (2 Kings 18:17–37; see also 2 Kings 19:10). In that real, historical situation, God delivered His people by the hand of the angel of the Lord (2 Kings 19:35, 26). In the fictional story of Judith, the agent of deliverance is Judith, a humble widow. She would prove once again that God can use the weak and despised to demonstrate His power and grace (see 1 Corinthians 1:27–31; the supreme illustration of this principle is the cross).

The harsh response of Holofernes in casting out Achior for his honesty (Judith 6:10) counterbalances the mercy of the Jews who take him in and offer him exemplary hospitality (6:20, 21). The irony, of course, is that Achior survives his expulsion from Holofernes's camp. Not only does he receive a merciful reception from the Jews, but he also ends up believing in God and converting to the Jewish faith (14:10).

The siege begins in chapter 7. Judith's original readers must have felt the same despair that the Israelites felt in 7:4 when considering the strength and size of the enemy forces they faced. With Egypt on the south and a variety of empires to the north, east, and west (Assyrian, Babylonian, Persian, Greek, Roman), God's people routinely found themselves between a rock and a hard place. Yet, trusting God, they prepare to defend their land (Judith 7:5). When Holofernes seizes the water supply, the enemy's victory seemed assured.

The residents of Bethulia believe their sins (and the sins of their ancestors) somehow led God to abandon them to Holofernes (7:23–28). Many of God's people who experienced suffering at the hand of Gentiles in the second century BC thought the same thing. Like the Hebrews in the wilderness of Sin (Exodus 17:1–7), the people of Bethulia would need a miracle to save them. Uzziah talks them into a five-day delay before they raise the white flag of surrender (Judith 7:29–31).

4 The Deliverer Appears *(Judith 8–9)*

Now Judith enters the picture (8:1). Her name means "Jewish woman," and she embodies the ideals of the Jewish culture in the second century BC. Beautiful and pious, smart and talented, capable of managing a large estate with many employees, Judith fasts every day except for the days when fasting is forbidden (8:6). She is the polar opposite of Holofernes in every respect. Her social position in Bethulia means that she can summon the male leadership of the town to her house and upbraid them (8:9–17).

Throughout Scripture, the Lord makes it clear that He rules the world He has created. He cannot be judged by mankind (as reflected in the Book of Job), nor does He operate by our timetable (as reflected in 2 Peter 3:1–12). Judith warns the leadership of her village against trying to dictate terms to God (Judith 8:11–17) and points out that their surrender will mean the destruction of the temple and the deaths of countless thousands of their countrymen. They would save their own lives only to find that their lives would not be worth living (8:18–23).

Judith's attitude toward the current crisis will sound familiar to readers of the New Testament. She challenges the town's leaders to give thanks for the desperate situation and consider it a test from the Lord (8:24–25; compare Philippians 4:4–6; 1 Thessalonians 5:16–18). God's tests not only reveal faith; they also strengthen faith (note her reference to Isaac; compare James 2:21; Hebrews 11:17–19). The suffering we endure may not make sense to us, but it makes sense to God, who has a holy purpose behind it (see Romans 8:28). The cross stands as the greatest example of something that looks terrible but serves a necessary purpose in God's plan of salvation, the very heart and core of it.

A pious warrior also knows the value of prayer, and so Judith prays in chapter 9. At the time of evening prayers in the temple, Judith comes before the Lord wearing ashes and revealing her sackcloth garments. Her faith and the temple's activities are in perfect synchronization. Her prayer begins with a reference to her ancestor Simeon, son of Jacob (compare her genealogy in 8:1 with Numbers 1:6). Simeon and his brother Levi had practiced deception and murdered the residents of Shechem (Genesis 34). To be fair, Shechem (the prince) had also acted deceitfully, planning to assimilate the smaller group of Jacob's family and property into their own community. Simeon and Levi sought vengeance for the violation of their sister Dinah (Genesis 34:7; compare Judith 9:2).

Jacob chastised his sons for their act of violence (Genesis 34:30) and later passed them over when he selected his son Judah as the one through whom the promise of a Savior would come (see Genesis 49:5–7). Judith evaluates their deceit and violence positively, not surprising in light of her own plans. Where Jacob had worried about the practical ramifications of the destruction of Shechem, Judith considered only the outrage perpetrated on Dinah and the attack on the family honor it represented.

She appeals to God's honor, acknowledging His power and her weakness (twice mentioning that she is a widow). The situation of the village is hopeless, but God is the "Savior of those without hope" (Judith 9:11).

5 The Lord Delivers His People *(Judith 10–16)*

Like Batman preparing for battle by donning his costume and utility belt, Judith prepares for her mission by undergoing a total transformation from pious Jewish widow to amazingly beautiful seductress (10:1–5). She and her sidekick, "the maid," then proceed through the gates, committing her plan to the Lord (10:8).

Although Judith practices deception with Holofernes throughout much of her speech, her comments in 11:16b ring true: "God has sent me to accomplish with you things that will astonish the whole word, as many as shall hear about them." The reader of the book, however, understands her point very differently than the fictional Holofernes (see also 12:18). Holofernes sees Judith making a complete conversion from her people, her culture, and her religion to his (keeping in mind both Holofernes and Judith are fictional characters). By faithful obedience to the Law, she overcomes the enemy, even though he is stronger.

Keeping kosher, as did Daniel in Babylon (Daniel 1:8), Judith sets the stage in chapter 12 for her ultimate return to Bethulia by night. She establishes a pattern of evening prayer outside the camp (keeping in mind she has only five days to accomplish her plan). Judith's plan depends on several things beyond her control: (a) no one will assault her and thus defile her (see 13:16); (b) Holofernes will arrange a "private meeting" with her alone (ch. 12); (c) Holofernes would pass out, rendering him defenseless and vulnerable (13:1–2). All this happens in this fictional work, mirroring God's work in the historical, biblical Book of Esther.

Judith resembles some of the outstanding women in the Old Testament, but she also differs from them. Like Esther, she is beautiful and her beauty wins her access to the key individual in the story. Unlike Esther, she feels no fear and shows no hesitation in approaching the story's key figure, even though it puts her life in jeopardy (see Esther 4:16). Also unlike Esther, she comes up with the plan herself.

Like Deborah, Judith demonstrated great faith and courage (see Judges 4). Unlike Deborah, she did not send a man to do the work. From the beginning, she planned to defeat the enemy herself. Like Jael (also Judges 4), she kills the enemy general. Unlike Jael, the opportunity to kill him didn't come suddenly. She planned and executed it intentionally.

Judith 13:1–10 records her success. The kosher food bag provides the necessary container for Holofernes's head; the previous evening prayers establish permission for her exit from the enemy camp. Undefiled, she returns to her village, praising God for the victory He has given her and His people (13:11). The people join her in worship (13:17), as does Uzziah (13:18). She offers a plan for the morning and secures the conversion of Achior (14:3–5), bringing together the stories of these two characters into one faith.

Conclusion

What may God's people today take away from the message of this book and the history that stands behind it? Shall we train our daughters as femme fatales, teach them to lie for a good cause, and put swords in their hands? These elements are important to the writer's plot and may even reflect the desperation people felt in the Time between the Testaments, abandoning their standards in an effort to save them! Not the best message.

However, several elements of the story ring true for us: keep God's Word, faith makes bold, and the Lord will preserve His people. These are truths to which we may cling today and always. As Jesus teaches, "the gates of hell shall not prevail against" the Church (Matthew 16:18).

Concluding Activities

Conclude the session with an appropriate prayer and distribute the study leaflet for week 9.

Wisdom Is Radiant and Unfading

Wisdom of Solomon

Preparing for the Session

Central Focus

"The fear of the Lord is the beginning of wisdom" (Psalm 111:10). Acknowledging the one true God and submitting in faith to Him serves as the foundation for living in this world and being welcomed into eternal life when we die.

Objectives

That participants, led by the Holy Spirit working through God's Word, will

1. see the folly in placing anything above God in their lives;
2. find encouragement to "keep the faith" in the face of worldly pressure to abandon it; and
3. rejoice that Jesus Christ, the wisdom and power of God, has opened the way to eternal life through His death and resurrection.

Note for the small-group leaders: Lesson notes and other materials you will need begin on page 71.

For the Lecture Leader

Session Plan

Worship

Begin the session with the hymn printed in the study leaflet. Accompaniments are available in denominational hymnals, such as *Lutheran Service Book* or *Lutheran Worship* (refer to hymnal index). (Note: Concordia Publishing House has available *The Concordia Organist*. All the initial worship hymns in the LifeLight courses are included in this resource. It's especially helpful for mission congregations and small parishes. See the list of study resources on p. 7.) Follow with this prayer:

Prayer

Father, keep us faithful through all the trials and temptations of this life. Anchor us by Your Holy Spirit in Jesus Christ, our Good Shepherd, so that the cares and pressures of this world do not distract or discourage us. Wipe away deception from our eyes and fear from our hearts, filling us with the spirit of power, love, and sound thinking we need to witness to You, the one true God. In Jesus' name. Amen.

Lecture Presentation

Introduction

As we saw in Sessions 2 through 4, the wisdom of Jesus son of Sirach circled back to various themes; we find a similar outcome in the Wisdom of Solomon. As with Ecclesiasticus, we will skip forward at times rather than comment on every passage.

The Wisdom of Solomon was most likely written by a Jewish author living in Alexandria, Egypt, sometime in the first half of the first century AD. The book encourages Jews to remain faithful to the one true God and to their Jewish heritage in spite of the allures and pressures of Gentile culture. Composed in Greek, the book reflects the author's familiarity with the Hebrew Scriptures, which he assumes his readers also know, and with Greek thinking (see chs. 8 and 9). Unlike many of the other books of the Apocrypha written in the second century BC, the audience of this book lives under Roman domination.

Jews living outside of Israel often faced local persecution as well as Roman oppression, a "double whammy" that made it very difficult to continue in the faith and traditions of their ancestors. A conflict between the Jews of Alexandria and their Gentile neighbors came to a head in AD 38, when riots broke out, ignited by virulent anti-Semitism. Philo of Alexandria, sometimes thought to be the author of the Wisdom of Solomon, led a delegation to the Roman emperor Caligula to address the situation. The situation there was so bad that Flaccus, the prefect (governor) of Alexandria, was eventually tried and executed for his part in the riots.

In a sense, conditions under the Romans had improved for the people of God in Israel. No longer did they find themselves in the middle of an ongoing struggle between the Ptolemies of Egypt and the Seleucids of Syria, nor did they face the turmoil of civil war as they had under Hasmonean rulers in the first and second centuries BC. Yet they still faced the hostility of Gentiles, the pressure to give up their faith and their identity, and the temptations offered by Roman culture. The players had changed but the game remained the same.

"Righteousness" plays a key role in the Wisdom of Solomon. The word group appears frequently in the Hebrew Scriptures and describes conformity to a certain standard, resulting in something that is reliable and trustworthy. A set of scales that accurately measures weight is "righteous" because it does what it is supposed to do (see Leviticus 19:36). Buyers and sellers can therefore trust the "righteous" scale.

For the child of God, "righteousness" does not describe adherence to a standard created by human beings. It refers to a life that conforms to God's own "righteousness" as revealed in His "righteous" decrees and laws. Even then, in the way the Scriptures use it, "righteousness" begins with a right relationship with God based on saving faith (see Genesis 15:6). True "righteousness" shows itself in charity, compassion, and consideration of others. Jesus makes this point when He criticizes the Pharisees for adhering to the letter of the Law of Moses while forsaking its spirit (Matthew 9:13; 12:7—citing Hosea 6:6; note also Habakkuk 2:4). Ultimately, only God is "righteous," and His "righteousness" makes Him utterly reliable and trustworthy because He cannot go back on His Word or fail to keep a promise (2 Timothy 2:13).

1 An Introduction to Two Paths *(Wisdom 1:1–4:19)*

In 1:1–15, the author begins his work by showing the value of righteousness versus wickedness. He addresses rulers in verse 1 but intends his advice for all of God's people. He begins by pointing out that trust functions as the foundation of a person's relationship to God (v. 2) so that even in difficult or uncertain times the child of God does not put the Lord to the test. Requiring God to "prove" His love for us flows from distrust. Satan often uses this approach when trying to separate God's people from Him, as with Adam and Eve in Genesis 3:1–6 (successfully) or as with Jesus in Matthew 4:5–7 (unsuccessfully). The path of wisdom is paved with trust in the Lord and obedience to His commands.

The other path, the way of the ungodly, initially looks like it will take the traveler to a nice place by a much easier route. Appearances, however, can be deceiving. As Asaph notes in Psalm 73, the end of every path is a reckoning. In Wisdom 1:6–11, the author reminds his readers that God will hold a person accountable for every word and every thought. Even though it might seem like foolishness and wickedness go unpunished in this life, God keeps track of everything. In reality, the path of wickedness leads to death (1:12–15). Only the path of righteousness leads to life.

The section from 1:16–2:20 portrays the reasoning of the wicked. They foolishly consider life an accident and death the end of life—but no more. Their motto in 2:1–9 might best be summed up in the quotation "Let us eat, drink, and be merry, for tomorrow we die." The same advice appears many centuries later in the work of Thomas Jordan, an English poet who lived from about AD 1612–85. He argued for a surplus of wine, women, and song in his poem "Let Us Drink and Be Merry." Paul reaches the same conclusion about life's purpose if there is no resurrection (1 Corinthians 15:32, quoting Isaiah 22:13). The author of Wisdom does a fair job of representing this self-indulgent approach to life.

The author of Wisdom exposes the thinking of the wicked in 2:10–20 as they plot against the righteous. The wicked respond negatively to the righteous who refuse to join them in their revelry (note 2:9). Anger turns to violence as they then oppress the faithful child of God, a theme common in the Psalms (see Psalm 69, especially vv. 7–9). The New Testament reminds us that the darkness of evil, no matter how strong, cannot overcome the light of Jesus Christ, who overcomes the world (see John 1:5; 3:19; 16:33).

The source of wickedness is identified in Wisdom 2:21–24, which makes clear to the reader where the path of sin leads. He refers to Genesis 1:26–28 and 3:1–6 to explain the source of foolish thinking (the devil), God's original purpose for humanity (life with Him), and the destiny of those who follow the devil's path of wickedness (death). The wicked seem to conquer the righteous by killing them, but the righteous enter the presence of God, experiencing eternal peace and joy (Wisdom 3:1–9). Not so the wicked, whose earthly accomplishments fall apart, leaving them with a shameful heritage (3:10–13). Scripture makes a similar point (see Psalms 1, 9, 10, 37, and many others).

Wisdom 3:14–4:19 contrasts the heritage of the wicked with the righteous. Ordinarily, children were considered a great blessing (see Psalm 128). However, the children of the wicked don't begin to compare to the heritage of the righteous, even if the righteous have no offspring (perhaps because they die before they can have families due to the persecution of the wicked; see Wisdom 4:13–15). The witness of the righteous and eternal life more than make up for lack of offspring.

2 The Value of Wisdom *(Wisdom 4:20–8:21)*

The author of Wisdom pictures the reaction of the wicked on the day of final judgment when they see the reward of the righteous (4:20–5:14). He points out that the lives of the unrighteous have had little or no impact on the world. He doesn't elaborate on the impact of the righteous in the present world but paints a vivid picture of their eternal reward (5:15–23). Perhaps drawing on Isaiah 59 (see especially v. 17), Wisdom depicts the judgment of the wicked with colorful brushstrokes here.

In Matthew 25:31–46, Jesus also reflects on the final judgment of the righteous and the wicked. Neither the sheep (the saved) nor the goats (the condemned) seem surprised at their eternal destination or the reasons for the sentence. They do show surprise when Jesus claims that their help (or lack thereof) involved Him personally. An English translation that reflects the emphasis of the original would be "Lord, when *You* did we see hungry . . ." (Matthew 25:37; see also v. 44).

The works of the righteous (an evidence of their living faith) leave a legacy because God cares about what happens to His children. Jesus takes personally what people do to His brothers (Christians), both positively and negatively. The wicked live only for themselves and end up with nothing. Those righteous by faith in Christ inherit the earth, for they have considered others before themselves (see Matthew 5:5; Philippians 2:4–11).

Having established the folly of wickedness and the wisdom of righteousness, the author then applies this lesson to the rulers in Wisdom 6:1–11 who make life so difficult for God's people. Officials who encourage or even tolerate the persecution of God's people (as in Alexandria in AD 38) will find themselves held accountable by the Lord.

The wisest man of all time, Solomon, enters the picture in chapter 7. In an effort to remind his royal readers of their humble beginnings, Wisdom pictures Solomon reflecting on his own conception and birth (vv. 1–6). He realizes that wisdom came to him as a gift from God (see 1 Kings 3:7–14). By means of that wisdom, he gained wealth (Wisdom 7:7–14) and an understanding of life and how it works (7:15–22). Ultimately, true wisdom always comes from God (7:23–8:1; see 1 Corinthians 1:24).

3 Wisdom Comes from God and Leads to God *(Wisdom 9–12)*

If "wisdom" may be defined as the insight that allows one to successfully navigate the course of life, then it serves as something of an "umbrella" virtue. A person who has wisdom will act prudently and cautiously, practice kindness and self-control, and acquire honor, wealth, power, prestige, and even the approval of God (ch. 10). Scripture testifies that the "fear of the Lord" is the beginning of wisdom; that is, a right relationship with God based on trust in Him and submission to His will. Human wisdom may gain human approval but the only evaluation that matters is God's judgment. As Hebrews notes, "Without faith it is impossible to please Him" (11:6). In Wisdom 9:5, the author depicts Solomon in humility, asking God for wisdom to rule the people and build the temple. He does not explicitly mention faith, as does the author of Hebrews, but he implies it in chapter 9.

We have already seen this author personify divine wisdom (for example, ch. 6), and he employs this figure of speech more fully in chapters 9 and 10. The reference to Adam (10:1–2) seems strange in light of Genesis 3:1–6. Eating the fruit of the forbidden tree, an act of unbelief and rebellion against God, constitutes the height of folly. Only the suffering and death of Jesus Christ on the cross delivered Adam (and all people) from transgression (see Romans 3:21–26). However, Adam did have a comprehensive understanding of the animal kingdom he ruled; naming the animals would include their characteristics and their places in the ecosystem. This "understanding in action" would count as "wisdom" as he continued to interact with God's creation after the fall.

Joseph's case also raises a few questions (Wisdom 10:13–14). If he had acted wisely, he might not have told his family his dreams, realizing they might stir up jealousy in his brothers and anger in his father (Genesis 37:10–11). Had he employed wisdom, he might not have gone alone when searching for his brothers, making him vulnerable to their anger (Genesis 37:12–19). He certainly acted wisely when he rejected the advances of Potiphar's wife (Genesis 39), choosing to obey God rather than give in to the pressure of her advances. His rescue from prison and rise to power, however, clearly comes directly from God (Genesis 41). The interpretation of the dreams, the presence of the Pharaoh's baker and cupbearer, and the timing of the cupbearer's revelation to Pharaoh have nothing to do with Joseph and everything to do with God. Only if we understand divine "wisdom" as a figure of speech for God Himself can we agree with the author about these verses.

Wisdom 10:15 continues to use "wisdom" in this way as the author considers the exodus. When God delivered His people from slavery in Egypt (Exodus 12), He not only fulfilled His promise to Abraham (Genesis 15:12–16) but also provided a preview of the cross (see Luke 9:30–31, where the word "departure" translates the Greek word "exodus"). Reconnecting to the greatest act of salvation in the Hebrew Scriptures also served as the focus for the Sabbath (Deuteronomy 5:15). The exodus and the wilderness experience of Israel will serve as the basis for the rest of the book.

4 The Folly of Idolatry and the Wisdom of God *(Wisdom 13:1–15:17)*

In 13:1–9, the author of Wisdom seems to limit the culpability of pagans for the sin of their idolatry (compare v. 6 with v. 18). Paul argues that the people who never heard the truth of the living God have no excuse for their idolatry since they should have figured out that they needed to worship the one invisible Creator rather than the creation (Romans 1:18–25). To the extent that they rejected the Creator revealed by His creation, their ignorance is culpable.

Wisdom paints a striking picture of idolatry's folly in 13:10–19, doubtless drawing on the Hebrew Scriptures for inspiration and imagery (see Isaiah 44:9–23; Jeremiah 10:1–10). He expands his criticism of idolatry by adding irony in the last several verses, which highlight the utter uselessness of idolatry. It may be likely that some idolaters understood that the idol merely represented the deity and was used as a "visual aid" for connecting to that deity. Perhaps some of the idols underwent a ceremony whereby a power or presence of the deity was infused into the idol. However, human nature tends to focus on concrete things and many, if not most, idolaters probably looked at the idol as an object of worship and prayer. Scripture offers a good example of this tendency in the account of when Hezekiah had the bronze serpent of Moses destroyed because people were worshiping it with incense and offerings (see 2 Kings 18:4; cf. Numbers 21:8–9). God had very good reasons for prohibiting graven images (Exodus 20:4–5).

What pagans credit to idols, God actually does in spite of their ignorance and for their own benefit (Wisdom 14:1–11). The wood used to make idols cannot help those who sail in ships of wood, but God has used wood to save people (for example, the ark of Noah; Genesis 6–9). Idols of wood become fatal traps for people because they promise help from sources other than the living God (see Isaiah 45:20; 57:13). Christians can affirm the truth of the statement "For blessed is the wood by which righteousness comes" (Wisdom 14:7). Although written with the ark of Noah in mind, it reminds Christians of the wooden cross on which our Savior died to save us from our sins.

Wisdom describes two sources of idolatry in 14:12–31. High infant mortality rates were common in the ancient world, as they are in some parts of the world today. The practice of creating an image of the deceased child, leading to idolatry, seems strange to us but would have been more natural in the ancient world—and also in many third-world countries today, due to the attitude the living have toward the dead. A modern example of this phenomenon is the "Day of the Dead" festival held in Mexico on November 1. The Day of the Dead may be traced to Aztec religious rituals honoring the departed.

The second source of idolatry described in this section developed from the practice of representing a distant monarch by means of a figurine or likeness. We practice something similar when we place portraits of political leaders in official buildings in our own country. In the ancient world, it would be easy to move from honoring that image to worshiping it, particularly since monarchs were thought to become gods upon their death.

Idols promise help but fail to deliver. Idols hold out the hope of eternal life only to utterly fail. In 15:1–17, Wisdom turns the reader's attention to the one true God as the only source of help and salvation. To know God is to have salvation, a point Paul made in Philippians 3:10. To know Christ is to share in His resurrection and to share in His sufferings.

5 Lessons from the Exodus *(Wisdom 15:18–19:22)*

In chapter 16, Wisdom turns to the incident where Israel spurned God's grace and, after God chastised them with poisonous snakes, repented (Numbers 21:4–9). The story in Numbers 21 begins with an Israelite victory over Arad (vv. 1–3). The confidence they feel from defeating Arad leads to dissatisfaction with God's command to bypass Edom (20:14–20). In their rebellion, the Israelites reject God's gracious provision of bread from heaven (21:5). Like Moses striking the rock (20:2–13), they rejected God by rejecting the symbol of His presence among them. As Adam and Eve learned in Genesis 3, rejecting God puts you in the hands of Satan, and only terrible things happen at that point.

In His mercy, the Lord limited the impact of the poisonous snakes. It was no doubt a shock to Moses and the Israelites when God directed Moses to make a bronze serpent that, when lifted up, would provide rescue for those who looked at it with faith in God. Jesus would later use this symbol of Satan's defeat to describe His crucifixion (see John 3:14–15; 12:31–32).

The author of Wisdom contrasts the purpose of the poisonous snakes (discipline) with that of the Ten Plagues (punishment) and the temporary duration of the serpent problem with the permanent impact of the tenth plague (death of the firstborn). Hebrews makes a similar point regarding the discipline of the Lord (Hebrews 12:5–11). Wisdom continues to contrast the punishment of the Egyptians (16:15–19) with the providence of God for the Israelites (16:20–29). Wisdom's original readers could apply these lessons to their own lives.

Wisdom focuses on the role of the high priest (Aaron) in saving the Israelites from God's judgment in 18:20–25, reflecting the importance of the high priest in Jerusalem for God's people in the second century BC until the fall of Jerusalem and its temple in AD 70. Only the high priesthood of Jesus continues permanently (see Hebrews 6:20).

Conclusion

In chapter 19, the author of Wisdom concludes his treatment of the consequences of idolatry for the Gentiles and the blessings of faith for the Israelites. Ultimately, he concludes, God always takes care of His people (v. 22). Christians will appreciate this affirmation, echoed in St. Paul's encouragement to believers of all times that "for those who love God all things work together for good" (Romans 8:28).

The author of Wisdom encourages his readers to bear patiently the persecution and troubles they face, trusting God to work out their salvation. Reminded by Scripture's record of the exodus, God's people understand that He alone saves them—even though He also does discipline them at times.

Concluding Activities

If possible, announce the next LifeLight course and encourage participants to register and invite others to participate also. Speak a prayer thanking God for the growth experienced during this course and for continued growth through His Word for all participants.

Small-Group Leaders Material

COVER: The three archangels with Tobias, by Francesco Botticini. Art Archive, The / Art Archive, The

Righteousness and Shame

Baruch; Letter of Jeremiah; Susanna

Preparing for the Session

Central Focus

In God's righteousness, He deals with sin by disciplining His people. The child of God responds by confessing all sin and turning to the wisdom of God for direction. Forgiven, God's people rejoice in their restoration accomplished in Christ Jesus.

Objectives

That participants, led by the Holy Spirit working through God's Word, will

1. seek the Lord in humility, confessing all sins and rejoicing in the full forgiveness won for us by Jesus Christ;

2. pray for others, especially leaders and the nation, that they might turn to the Lord and walk the path of wisdom; and

3. turn to the Lord in prayer and trust His Word when faced with trial or temptation.

For the Small-Group Leader

Small-Group Discussion Helps

Day 1 • Read Baruch 1:1–2:26

1. Jeremiah 36:4 says Baruch, the son of Neriah, served as Jeremiah's scribe. Baruch 1:1 names four other of Baruch's ancestors and that he wrote while in exile at Babylon.

2. The author is encouraging the Judeans to repent of the sins that caused God to send them into exile. He also prays for deliverance from captivity.

3. They had the need for God to turn His anger away from them, as they were few in number, and answer their prayers so they might have relief from distress, hunger, and feebleness.

4. Answers may vary. Comments might include the fact that God is ever ready to hear the prayers of those who repent. He may intervene in even the most desperate circumstances and even when He brought those circumstances about to punish the people.

5. *For personal reflection. Sharing optional.* Answers will vary. You might invite participants to share an example, if someone is willing. Those struggling over sin should be encouraged to go to either corporate confession in the worship service or private confession with their pastor or a trusted confessor. Assure the group that when we ask God's forgiveness, He provides it and we need not perpetually ask forgiveness for things forgiven (Psalm 103:12).

Day 2 • Read Baruch 2:27–4:4

6. The passage from Baruch echoes texts in Deuteronomy and Jeremiah about God giving people a new heart through repentance. God will remember the covenant He made with their father Abraham.

7. The style changes from prose to poetry, which may or may not be immediately evident, depending on the English translation being read.

8. The beginning of the passage sounds like Solomon's counsel in Proverbs. Jacob is mentioned as a hero who received God's wisdom (3:36). The passage ends by commending Israel to God's Word.

9. (a) The author of Baruch sought wisdom. (b) He described this wisdom as the way of God, strength, understanding, treasure from God's house, a woman who appeared to Israel, and the book of God's commandments.

Day 3 • Read Baruch 4:5–5:9

10. The author called God's people the "memorial of Israel" (4:5); "Zion" (4:9); "my sons and daughters" (4:10); "a widow" (4:12); "a flock" (4:26); "Jerusalem" (4:30); "Peace of righteousness and glory of godliness" (5:4); and "Israel" (5:7).

11. They are most likely Judeans or persons devoted to the Jerusalem temple, though they also would lay claim to the broader heritage of "Israel," as Jews did in the Time between the Testaments and still do. They feel like a widow or like lost children, since they are in exile. They still perhaps see themselves as children of God.

12. "God" (beginning at 4:6); "the everlasting God" (4:8); "the Everlasting" (beginning at 4:10); "Holy One" (beginning at 4:22); "everlasting Savior" (4:22).

13. The author emphasizes God's everlasting nature, that the Lord is not limited like the earthly leaders who failed the people. He also writes about God's holiness. Perhaps surprisingly, "Holy One" is not a threatening title but one associated with joy and restoration. Indeed, He is the writer's Savior.

14. (a & b) Answers will vary. Participants may choose titles from the reading, from Scripture, or even of their own creation. Encourage participants to think carefully about how they describe themselves and the Lord in their prayers. Draw on the variety in Scripture and in good devotional literature for a deeper prayer life.

Day 4 • Read the Letter of Jeremiah

15. *For personal reflection. Sharing optional.* The author wishes to point out the follies of idolatry to the Judean captives in Babylon to deter them from falling into false worship.

16. The author uses irony and humor to point out the foolishness of idol worship. Overall, the letter is somewhat repetitive.

17. (a & b) Answers will vary. Allow some participants to share their insights.

18. God's people continued to feel the need to set things right with God through repentance. They clearly felt intimidated in the presence of foreigners, an unclean culture, and idolatry.

Day 5 • Read Susanna

19. The story takes place during the Babylonian exile and in Babylon. The source of inspiration is the Book of Daniel, as that prophet is mentioned in verse 45.

20. Captivity, corrupt leadership, feelings of defenselessness, and weaknesses of the legal system.

21. Answers may vary but may include the theme of marital faithfulness, the sound use of wisdom and prayer, and the virtue of standing up for what is right despite the conclusions of the crowd.

22. God works through the wisdom of young Daniel, who grew suspicious of the corrupt elders.

23. Sometimes, perhaps often, we cannot rescue ourselves but must depend upon the kindness of others, which calls for patience. God invites us to trust that He will hear our prayers. Paul tells us in Romans that nothing can separate us from God's love or bring about our condemnation when we are in Christ. Such promises inspire in us great trust for the Lord.

Gloriously Reveal the Works of God

Tobit; Ecclesiasticus 1:1–6:17

Preparing for the Session

Central Focus

All good gifts come from God (James 1:17), though God's people also experience suffering in this sin-broken world.

Objectives

That participants, led by the Holy Spirit working through God's Word, will

1. appreciate God's gifts and thank Him for them daily;
2. understand better the value of suffering for God's people; and
3. see the importance of wisdom and the third use of the Law as guides in daily life.

For the Small-Group Leader

Small-Group Discussion Helps

Day 1 • Read Tobit 1–3

1. The story takes place following the Assyrian conquest of Israel, after 722 BC but before the fall of Nineveh to the Medes and Babylonians in 612 BC. Tobit was taken from the region of Naphtali (Galilee) to Nineveh. It also describes business travel to Media and later Ecbatana. Events include the captivity and exile, the breaking away of the northern tribes from Judah and the Jerusalem sanctuary, Tobit's promotion, and business travel.

2. The author describes how some people from the northern tribes continued to go to the temple in Jerusalem despite the schism under Rehoboam (931 BC) and the sin of Jeroboam, who introduced the worship of golden calves. Tobit's travels to Jerusalem may describe the later restoration of fellowship that happened under Hezekiah.

3. Tobit describes defying Assyrian law in order to bury his countrymen. He also fed the poor. His motive was to continue in the practices of God's Word. Tobit expresses sincere faith in the Lord through devotion to Old Testament practices. He trusts in God's mercy (3:2–3).

4. By keeping God's commands, Tobit revealed that he was a foreigner who disobeyed the emperor. Anna could see no advantage in the mercy that Tobit expressed toward fellow Israelites in keeping with God's Word.

5. Paul recognizes that, despite our suffering, God still has purposes for us in this life. Paul, like Tobit and Sarah, was ready to die but still sought God's will always.

Day 2 • Tobit 4–8

6. Although Tobit suffered for keeping God's Word, he still encouraged his son, Tobias, to keep God's Word and to act charitably toward others. This reveals Tobit's deep commitment to the Lord and to His ways.

7. (a) God does promise to bless those who keep His Word. (b) God's promise is not meant as a guarantee that things will always go well for us. The righteous may suffer loss, as did the Hebrews in a time of persecution.

8. (a) The angel Raphael, who introduces himself as Azarias, son of Ananias. (b) The angel also agrees to travel with Tobias. (c) His accompaniment of Tobias fulfills Tobit's prayer for someone to go with his son. It sets in motion a complete vindication of Tobias's views.

9. Raphael tells Tobias he will stay with Raguel, marry Sarah, gain rights to her inheritance, and drive a demon from the bridal chamber by burning the heart and liver of a fish so he and Sarah may live happily ever after!

10. **Challenge question.** Elements included in the story: (1) The matchmaker discusses a bride with the groom. (2) The potential groom and matchmaker visit with the parents and potential bride at their home. (3) The bride's family provides a meal for the potential groom, matchmaker, and father. (4) The groom asks the matchmaker to negotiate the marriage. (5) The matchmaker suggests to the father a marriage. (6) The matchmaker discusses inheritance with the father. (7) The father gives away his daughter, the bride. (8) The father gives his blessing. (9) The groom and father of the bride make a binding agreement/contract. (10) The parents of the bride set their seal on the contract. (11) They all feast. (12) The mother prepares the bride and bridal chamber. (13) The groom is escorted to the bridal chamber on the wedding night. (14) The father of the bride gives a fourteen-day wedding feast. (15) The father of the bride

gives the groom a gift of property and a promise of full inheritance. The text also mentions the ideal of marrying within one's tribe and levirate marriage, based on the Law of Moses. It is not clear whether an Israelite marriage always included all of these practices. They may have been common for marriages during the Time between the Testaments. Also, some elements may have been unique to the unusual circumstances of this marriage. Nevertheless, the story provides a detailed look at Israelite customs and rites surrounding marriage.

Day 3 • Read Tobit 9–12

11. First, Raguel kept his promises regarding the marriage. He spoke some form of benediction or prayer over the couple, although those words were not recorded (10:11). He promised them that God would prosper them and told Sarah to honor her new in-laws as her parents. Tobit welcomed Sarah (11:17) and then spoke a benediction toward God for bringing Sarah into the family. He also asked God's blessing upon her parents.

12. *For personal reflection. Sharing optional.* Answers will vary but should include spiritual blessings such as forgiveness, life, and salvation or blessings like those Paul prayed for in Ephesians 3:14–21. They may also include thanks for God's blessings upon body and life, as Raguel and Tobit gave thanks in the story. Thinking of God's blessings in view of the persons and work of the Holy Trinity can help you organize and enrich your prayers.

13. Answers may vary but should include the point that God condemns and forbids such magical rites and would have us come to Him in prayer directly.

14. **Challenge question.** Answers may vary but may include the following elements: angels may appear in human form (5:4–5); angels can lie (5:12–13); angels have names (5:4); angels know magic arts that drive out demons and bring healing (chs. 6; 8; 11); angels know the Law and can negotiate (6:11–13); angels may see the future (ch. 6); angels bind demons (8:3); angels praise God, encourage humans to do so as well, and speak wise sayings (12:6–22); angels can disappear (12:21); the title "angel of the Lord" may be applied to more than one specific angel (12:22). *Note well that some points in Tobit are contrary to passages in Scripture.*

15. Although God commanded almsgiving and commends it to us as a means of blessing others and receiving likewise the joy of giving (Acts 20:35), it does not take away sins. Sins are forgiven only through the sacrifice of Jesus Christ upon the cross. He grants us such a blessing through His Word and Sacraments. Perhaps almsgiving delivers from death if others repay a kindness in a time of need, one person helping another.

Day 4 • Read Tobit 13–14

16. God afflicts and shows mercy; He leads down to Hades and brings up again (13:2).

17. Tobit's thanks here focuses on Jerusalem, blessed by God (in His presence at the temple and ultimately through the visitation of Christ). From there, God would distribute His Word and blessings to all people.

18. **Challenge question.** The people did return from captivity and rebuild Jerusalem. However, not all Gentiles turned to the Lord and gave up their idols. Tobit anticipates something like the fulfillment of the new covenant described in Jeremiah 31 and the new Jerusalem in Isaiah 2, but these are fulfilled through Christ rather than a new temple building (cf. John 2:19).

19. Tobit recalls the importance of proper burial. The Israelites forced into exile saw many of their countrymen die in battle or die on the road to exile where they would have been left unburied. The orderly rites of a funeral are a great blessing for those who grieve. The Israelites wanted that blessing restored to them.

20. Answers will vary depending upon the needs and interests of participants. Allow some to share their thoughts about the beauty or content of the prayers and praises, which could be adapted for our prayers today.

Day 5 • Read Ecclesiasticus 1:1–6:17

21. The book was intended to provide wisdom to those who wished to know more about God's Law and how to live by it. It was to serve both Jews and Gentiles.

22. The Lord has supplied you with wisdom, which you may learn and gain through His creation.

23. (a) They are those who fear the Lord. (b) This does not mean to cower and hide from God but to trust in Him (cf. 2:16–17; Psalm 130:4).

24. By showing mercy to widows and orphans. Although these are among the noblest good works a person may do in outward righteousness, they do not purify the heart and mind as does Holy Baptism.

25. *For personal reflection. Sharing optional.* Answers will vary as participants choose words that most apply to them and how they see themselves in relation to God and others. Invite some to share their thoughts; emphasize the joy God takes in showing mercy and imparting wisdom through faith in Jesus Christ.

The Lord's Great Mercy

Ecclesiasticus 6:18–33:19

Preparing for the Session

Central Focus

In the same way a travel guide might offer a tourist advice on making his way through a foreign country, Jesus son of Sirach instructs his students on how to successfully navigate through life, applying wisdom (especially the Word of God) to everyday living.

Objectives

That participants, led by the Holy Spirit working through God's Word, will

1. learn the nature and value of true wisdom in their lives;

2. appreciate that women were created in the image of God and that those who believe are co-heirs in Christ; and

3. rejoice in the promise of eternal life in Christ regardless of the circumstances and situations they face in this life.

For the Small-Group Leader

Small-Group Discussion Helps

Day 1 • Read Ecclesiasticus 6:18–9:16

1. As did Solomon, Jesus son of Sirach describes wisdom as a woman because the Hebrew word for *wisdom* is feminine (cf. Proverbs 8:1–11). However, he then writes about wisdom enslaving a person (Ecclesiasticus 6:24–25)!

2. He writes about the importance of a good wife and obedient children. He describes honor for one's parents. In nearby passages, he also writes about servants, who could be members of the household.

3. (a) Jesus son of Sirach's proverbs thus far are predominately negative, "Do not . . ." He focuses on avoiding evil and not making mistakes. (b) He seems more prepared to write in this way than about what one should pursue and discover in life and service before God.

4. He speaks positively about a good wife (7:19, 26), worriedly about the chastity of a daughter (7:24), and negatively about women generally (9:1–9) due to temptations or potential scandal.

5. Jesus son of Sirach would focus his reader and his conversation upon God's Law, which would be God's instruction (both Law and Gospel theologically). Paul describes the preached and taught Word as God's very Word, which works in our lives, encourages us, and makes us worthy of the Lord.

Day 2 • Read Ecclesiasticus 9:17–14:19

6. Pride leads to sin, away from the Lord, and to abominations. All this results in God's condemnation.

7. The Ecclesiasticus passage is remarkably similar to Jesus' parable of the rich fool. Both texts illustrate the dangers of prideful independence, selfishness, and an inability to control one's life.

8. Jesus of Nazareth teaches that one can win people through kindness and mercy. This wisdom is opposite to that taught by Jesus son of Sirach.

9. *For personal reflection. Sharing optional.* Answers will vary depending on the experience and insight of the participants. Allow some to share their perspective for discussion. Avoid negative discussions of leaders, which is not the point of the question.

10. Jesus son of Sirach remarks often on the permanence of death. In contrast, Christians hope for the resurrection to life everlasting and can live each day joyfully in that hope, praying for the Son of God to return soon.

Day 3 • Read Ecclesiasticus 14:20–20:31

11. He describes wisdom both as a mother to the person who fears the Lord and as a young bride. The combination seems odd but seems to depend on the idea that wisdom feeds and supports someone, which would have been among the responsibilities of mothers and brides in that culture.

12. He makes clear that God is not responsible for sin, since He hates sin and would not create a sinful person. The writer puts the blame on human beings and misuse

of our freedom. One should note that since the fall into sin, sinners do not have a truly free will. That doctrine is an example of Greek philosophy influencing Jesus son of Sirach.

13. He describes the destructive influence of ungodly children upon Jerusalem, though he does not make clear whether they were his children or other people's children. He advises that it is better to have no children than to have ungodly children.

14. He refers to the Nephilim (Genesis 6:4), the people of Sodom and Gomorrah (Genesis 19), the Canaanites and other nations of the conquest (Joshua), and the host of Israel who rebelled against the Lord in the wilderness (e.g., Exodus 32).

15. Answers will vary but should include some description of the vastness of God's mercy toward sinners or a comparison like that found in Psalm 103:12 or Jesus' parables of Luke 15.

Day 4 • Read Ecclesiasticus 21:1–27:29

16. The lawless cause incurable wounds, whereas the Lord uses His sword to discern our thoughts and intentions. He applies judgment with merciful intent.

17. Answers may vary. Fools reveal their ill intent through what they say. The wise also reveal themselves with their words but with a righteous heart, which leads to prudent speech.

18. Jesus son of Sirach sometimes writes as though he experienced disappointment with his children and may have struggled to forgive them.

19. *For personal reflection. Sharing optional.* Answers may vary. Participants may share experiences of struggling to control their speech, passions, or other aspects of life.

20. The New Testament emphasizes the value of a bride to her husband in ways that go far beyond the few complimentary statements in Ecclesiasticus. For example, Jesus son of Sirach expresses thanks for what a good wife can do for her husband, whereas Paul writes about a husband sacrificing himself for his wife.

Day 5 • Read Ecclesiasticus 27:30–33:19

21. Slander leads to exile and destruction.

22. Answers may vary. He offers sound advice about the kindness and restraint good neighbors show toward one another.

23. Water, bread, clothing, and home.

24. Bodily needs are met, with the exception of sound sleep. There are also opportunities to be generous. However, insomnia, straying from faithfulness, and stumbling are potential curses from wealth.

25. *For personal reflection. Sharing optional.* Answers will vary. Allow participants to share thoughts, especially about spiritual provisions (forgiveness, life, and salvation in Christ).

The Blessed Fear the Lord

Ecclesiasticus 33:20–51:30

Preparing for the Session

Central Focus

Jesus son of Sirach guides travelers on the journey of life by celebrating the God-blessed accomplishments of earlier believers.

Objectives

That participants, led by the Holy Spirit working through God's Word, will

1. grow to love other people, including our enemies, as God loves us;

2. praise God, the creator and sustainer of the universe; and

3. praise God, the author and director of the plan of salvation that finds its fulfillment in Jesus Christ.

For the Small-Group Leader

Small-Group Discussion Helps

Day 1 • Read Ecclesiasticus 33:20–36:31

1. Jesus son of Sirach gives both the right and the wrong of a situation, which helps the reader more fully understand the consequences of his actions. Stating both makes things most clear.

2. Jesus son of Sirach shows the importance of repentance as an essential feature of offerings in the Old Testament. Without repentance and faith, the offering is an offense to God rather than something He welcomes. He also shows that acts of kindness are as welcome to God as the offerings He commands.

3. Both texts encourage humility, faithfulness, and persistence. These attributes speak to our attitudes in worship, through which we appeal to God, who sees our hearts and lives clearly.

4. Jesus son of Sirach envisions the return of Israel from exile and the filling of the Jerusalem temple.

5. Although other passages in Ecclesiasticus are surprisingly negative toward women, this passage describes a wife as the one who makes the home, makes life tolerable, and settles a man into a positive, productive life.

Day 2 • Ecclesiasticus 37:1–39:11

6. One should heed a godly man whose soul is in agreement with one's soul and who complements one's heartfelt plans. The Lord is the very best counselor, who generously has given us His Word. One should avoid a counselor who serves himself, is jealous, or is rivalrous.

7. God, physicians, medicines, pharmacists, prayer and offerings in prayer, as well as clean living were available at this time.

8. Answers may vary. The mourning seems a bit fake, since it is designed to escape others' criticism. On the other hand, he counsels well about how to avoid despair or depression that result from sorrow.

9. **Challenge question.** As a leading Jewish teacher, Jesus son of Sirach is obviously familiar with the natural, realistic painting style that was preferred in those days. He does not condemn such art but describes it positively. Here is literary evidence that helps one understand how Jews of this era interpreted Exodus 20:3–6. They regarded it as a prohibition against idols rather than against pictures.

10. He commends a scholarly or academic life, perhaps because his students will be in such training. He obviously regards this as the best way of life.

Day 3 • Read Ecclesiasticus 39:12–42:14

11. God is all-powerful and all-knowing. His will is ultimately done. Creation serves the good of those who honor the Creator but will work against the ungodly. He sees natural disasters as the works of God's vengeance. God's works are all good and cause for us to praise Him.

12. Answers will vary. Many points seem valid, although stating that one thing is better than another is not helpful if God intended both of them for our good (e.g., God commends having both a spouse and children). Ecclesiasticus 40:26b seems to teach that those who fear the Lord will escape all loss. This would contradict the Book of Job, though it could stand as a general observation, as do similar statements in Proverbs.

13. Paul does not celebrate or welcome death but celebrates the resurrection and God's gift of everlasting life.

14. Answers may vary but should note that shame is appropriate when one sins and that the removal of shame is a blessing that should leave one with proper humility and modesty.

15. False. This is a wickedly prejudiced statement that contradicts God's creation of Eve for Adam's benefit.

Day 4 • Ecclesiasticus 42:15–46:20

16. The beauty and blessing of creation.

17. This phrase might be misunderstood to teach pantheism, as though creation is God. One could rightly understand it to mean that the Lord is all-important, since His Word holds all creation together.

18. This section of Ecclesiasticus lists examples of people from the Old Testament and the Time between the Testaments, and it celebrates what the Lord did through them. As the previous section celebrated creation, this section celebrates His creation of a faithful people.

19. (a) The figure left out is Adam. (b) Adam may have been skipped because his decisions led to the fall into sin rather than to blessing.

20. (a) No one receives more attention in this section of the book than Aaron. (b) This is likely because he was the first high priest. After the return from exile, the high priest, rather than prophets or kings, was the most important leader.

Day 5 • Read Ecclesiasticus 47–51

21. It blesses those who saw Elijah, a prophet who was taken alive up to heaven. "We also shall surely live" may express hope in the resurrection and life in heaven that Elijah enjoyed.

22. This king and prophet were closely bound together in the history of Israel. Hezekiah followed the counsel God gave through Isaiah.

23. (a) Simon son of Onias. (b) He was the high priest at the time of Jesus son of Sirach, the most important leader in the land.

24. The prayer is a sincere, theologically correct expression of faith that believers today could use with confidence.

25. Answers will vary but will put the focus upon Jesus Christ. For example, one might write, "May your soul rejoice in Jesus' mercy, and may you not be put to shame when you praise Him. Do your work before Judgment Day, and when Jesus returns He will give you your reward" (cf. 51:29–30).

Additions to Holy Scripture

Old Greek Esther; Prayer of Manasseh; Prayer of Azariah; The Song of the Three Holy Children; Bel and the Dragon

Preparing for the Session

Central Focus

Even though the Bible might not answer every question we have or doesn't include information about something we wish it did, the Holy Spirit inspired the text to fulfill God's good purposes for His Church.

Objectives

That participants, led by the Holy Spirit working through God's Word, will

1. learn that God is always at work "behind the scenes" for the salvation of people;

2. know that, even in the midst of the crucible of suffering, God is with them; and

3. appreciate the worthlessness of false gods, and thus keep faith with the one true God.

For the Small-Group Leader

Small-Group Discussion Helps

Day 1 • Read Old Greek Esther 11:2–13:18 or the following major additions to the book: 11:2–12; ch. 12; 13:1–7; 13:8–18

1. Mordecai saw two dragons fighting, which brought distress to a righteous nation. Mordecai realized the dream was from God and sought to understand it.

2. Mordecai overheard a plot against the king and reported the two eunuchs who were planning it. The honor Mordecai received from the king caused Haman to be jealous.

3. The Judeans had laws contrary to those of other nations, and they disregarded the ordinances of the kings, which caused divisions in the kingdom.

4. Mordecai did not want to set the glory of man above the glory of God; he would not bow down to anyone but the Lord.

5. Israel was the Lord's inheritance: He redeemed them from Egypt, and they praised the Lord.

Day 2 • Read Old Greek Esther 14:1–11:1 or the following major additions to the book: chs. 14–15; ch. 16; 11:1; read also the Prayer of Manasseh

6. (a) Titles for God in Esther's prayer include "my Lord," "our King," "King of the gods," "Master of all dominion," "Lord God of Abraham," and "God." (b) Esther said she abhorred like a menstrual rag the sign of her proud position; her words are intended to show her humility and her indifference toward Gentile culture.

7. When the king looked at her in anger, she faltered, turned pale, fainted, and then collapsed. God worked through this to change the attitude of the king.

8. Changes Artaxerxes prescribed include making peace for all subjects, judging equitably, halting the actions Haman requested, permitting the Judeans to live under their law, letting the Jews defend themselves, and observing a commemorative festival about these events.

9. The prayer focuses on God's power as creator as well as on His mercy toward those who repent.

10. They describe the feelings of helplessness that the exiles felt as well as the continued sense of guilt associated with the exile. They were looking for God to be a merciful king over them who would rule them through His Law.

Day 3 • Read Daniel 3:13–23 and the Prayer of Azariah

11. The Prayer of Azariah explains what Azariah and the others were doing while they were in the midst of their troubles—a lively example for us to follow during times of trouble.

12. God was true and just, even when Israel sinned.

13. It appeals to God's covenant, His mercy, and His relationship with Abraham.

14. Israel has been brought low through sin, defeat, and exile. They had no political or spiritual leaders. They were also unable to offer sacrifices.

15. The author wanted to put to shame those who harmed Israel so they would know His glorious worldwide authority. In contrast, Jesus announced to the disciples that He would use His worldwide authority to bring salvation to the nations, and He sent the disciples forth for that purpose.

Day 4 • Read the Song of the Three Holy Children

16. The angel drove the fiery flame out of the furnace so that the midst of the furnace was like a moist wind.

17. This portion of the prayer addresses God ("you") directly, praising Him. The rest of the prayer appeals to others, telling them to bless the Lord. Note: You can see a modern version of the Song of the Three Holy Children in *Lutheran Service Book* 930, 931.

18. The Israelites commend blessing from the very things—fire and heat—that the Babylonians intended would destroy them.

19. Hierarchy: sons of men, Israel, priests, servants, spirits and souls of the righteous, humble and holy of heart. The list narrows from mankind generally to the priests and servants of the Lord who have a God-pleasing character.

20. Answers will vary. The prayer illustrates the faith of persecuted and suffering people who were able to think beyond their circumstances to the heavenly and earthly glories of God. Lord, help us to focus outward and upward on the good, perfect, and holy.

Day 5 • Read Bel and the Dragon

21. Daniel is invited to prove that Bel is a false god under penalty of death if he fails.

22. The priests of Bel had a secret passage that would allow them to sneak into the temple at night and consume the offering. Daniel had confidence in the living God as well as a plan to reveal the deceptions of the priests.

23. At the temple, he sprinkled ashes on the floor, which revealed the footprints of the priests. For the dragon, he prepared an indigestible cake that burst open the dragon. In both cases, Daniel made use of his God-given reason to overcome his opponents.

24. The lions were starved to make them ravenous, but Daniel is the one who gets fed. In the end, the ravenous lions ate those who had starved them.

25. God remembers us and will not forsake us (Joshua 1:5), since He loves us.

Reverence the Divine Laws

2 Maccabees

Preparing for the Session

Central Focus

God's people highly value commitment to the Lord and His teaching—even in the face of persecution. The Lord often works through hardship to deliver His people from evil.

Objectives

That participants, led by the Holy Spirit working through God's Word, will

1. understand the importance of the temple in God's plan of salvation;

2. recognize the importance of suffering in the outworking of God's plan of salvation; and

3. understand that Jesus, by His incarnation, replaces the temple and, by His death, ends the sacrificial system connected to it.

For the Small-Group Leader

Small-Group Discussion Helps

Day 1 • Read 2 Maccabees 1–3

1. The Babylonians removed the temple furniture and destroyed the temple in 586 BC, which defiled the site. The writer of the letter mentions "Persia" (1:19) rather than Babylon, likely because that later empire was better known to his readers.

2. Before the exile, pious priests had preserved the temple fire through a store of naphtha, which was ignited by God's creation—the sun—rather than by human hands.

3. Chapter 2 describes how Jeremiah preserved the altar fire and hid the tent (tabernacle), ark, and altar of incense.

4. The book was written to preserve the heroic story of the Maccabees and the restoration of the temple and Jerusalem. It is a condensation of a larger work by Jason of Cyrene that is otherwise lost.

5. The Lord sent an angelic rider of frightening appearance, whose horse struck down Heliodorus. Onias, the priest, then interceded for Heliodorus, who was not supposed to enter the temple.

Day 2 • Read 2 Maccabees 4–6

6. (a) Hellenization was the spread and intermixing of Greek culture with the Asian and Egyptian cultures. (b) Hellenization was the policy of Alexander the Great that was practiced by his successors, such as the Seleucids, and local officials, such as Jason.

7. Onias exposed the fact that Menelaus had stolen gold vessels from the temple and had given them to a Gentile.

8. Two rumors led Antiochus to Jerusalem. First, Jason falsely heard that Antiochus was dead and so stormed Jerusalem in an attempted coup. Second, Antiochus heard about the attempted coup and falsely assumed Judea was in revolt, which led him to attack Jerusalem.

9. God was, through Antiochus, punishing the leaders of Jerusalem who had profaned the temple and the city through hellenization and corruption.

10. The Lord uses these punishments to discipline His people. He works more patiently with the Gentiles, but swiftly with Israel, so that He might not destroy them if their sins would reach their fullest extent. More positively, "He never withdraws His mercy from us" (2 Maccabees 6:16).

Day 3 • Read 2 Maccabees 7–9

11. *For personal reflection. Sharing optional.* Answers will vary. These shocking accounts of torture cannot help but move God's people who themselves are called to follow God's Word.

12. The seven brothers bore witness to God's compassion, everlasting life, judgment upon Israel's sin, and judgment upon the sin of their tormentors. The seventh son interceded for Israel. In short, they bore witness both to God's Law and to His Gospel, compassion and forgiveness.

13. She urged her youngest son to steadfastly follow God's Word in the hope of the resurrection.

14. Hebrews likely refers to these martyrs in 2 Maccabees, who join their testimony to the faithful of the Old Testament. Their faith and bravery are examples from which we learn what it is to serve the Lord.

15. (a) Judas Maccabeus, who organized the revolt against the Seleucids and their Judean supporters. (b) He led the people in prayer for victory and also led them into battle, bringing victories against superior forces.

Day 4 • Read 2 Maccabees 10–12

16. The prayers asked to never again have such misfortune and requested discipline with forbearance. After they replaced the altar, they sacrificed, offered incense, relit the lampstand, set out the bread of the Presence, bowed in prayer, and held an eight-day celebration (like the Feast of Booths) that became the annual holiday of Hanukkah.

17. The Maccabees depended upon the Lord for their strength, received help from angelic riders, and acted with righteous anger. The Seleucids depended on their rage, their stronghold, and blasphemous curses.

18. At first, Lysias concluded that the Israelites were invincible because God fought for them, causing him to desire peace. However, the letter from the Romans reveals further motivation, since the Jews had a new ally that would have intimidated the Seleucids.

19. The Lord is described as the righteous judge, helper of the Judeans, sovereign of the world who willed the Judeans' victory. He reveals what is hidden and frees people from sin through atonement.

20. **Challenge question.** Judas sought to offer prayers and sacrifices for Judeans who had already died. Hebrews 9:27 does not allow for repentance and atonement after death, nor can a believer repent for another person. God calls each person to repentance and faith (2 Corinthians 6:2).

Day 5 • Read 2 Maccabees 13–15

21. Judas was pious, wise, brave, and inspirational, leading his troops in devotion to the Lord. Similar to a prophet, Judas received "a sort of vision."

22. Alcimus was duplicitous and seeking his own advantage, a friend to himself. Nicanor was favorably impressed with Judas, and made a covenant seeking peace with him. Nevertheless, when pressed, he too became duplicitous and an enemy toward Judas.

23. Answers may vary. However, suicide should not be praised as a noble choice, since God calls us to faith rather than despair. The martyrs of chapters 6–7 died nobly.

24. He saw the high priest Onias and an older man, Jeremiah, who was interceding for Israel. Jeremiah gave Judas a golden sword for defeating his enemies.

25. Answers will vary. The book certainly includes historic examples of faith and devotion that are inspiring. Yet it likewise includes examples of false doctrine and practice. For that reason, one must use it very carefully.

Strength Comes from Heaven

1 Maccabees

Preparing for the Session

Central Focus

Like Phinehas in Numbers 25, the Maccabees show such zeal for the name of the Lord in the face of Gentile opposition that God's wrath against His people ceases and they resecure for themselves the priesthood.

Objectives

That participants, led by the Holy Spirit working through God's Word, will

1. see the Lord is at work in history to accomplish His goal, the salvation of souls;
2. understand the nature of the "abomination of desolation" and its connection to the end times; and
3. appreciate the connection between the period of the Maccabees and the ministry of Jesus.

For the Small-Group Leader

Small-Group Discussion Helps

Day 1 • Read 1 Maccabees 1–2

1. The Book of 1 Maccabees begins with the conquests of Alexander the Great, Antiochus Epiphanes, and Mattathias's rebellion.

2. It describes the Gentile conquest of Jerusalem and desecration of the temple when they set up their sacrifices there (1:54).

3. Answers may vary. It is a poem of lamentation that shows the depth of offense and near despair Mattathias experienced. This explains why he was so willing to oppose the Gentiles with open rebellion.

4. In Exodus, Moses and the Levites slew those who persisted in worship of the golden calf. In Numbers, Phinehas zealously killed an Israelite prince caught up in impurity with a Moabitess. In 1 Samuel, those who rebelled against Saul gathered to David.

5. *For personal reflection. Sharing optional.* Answers will vary. Let several participants share their thoughts as time and good discussion allows. Emphasize God's favor toward His faithful who call us to similar faithfulness.

Day 2 • Read 1 Maccabees 3–5

6. Judas attributed success in battle to "heaven" (i.e., God; 3:18, 60). He believed that following God's Word and ways would lead to success (3:2–22).

7. The Gentiles consulted their idols, while the Jews consulted God's Word and called on the Lord through prayers and offerings. Christians today may follow the example of Judas and his troops, though one should be careful not to treat the Word as a divining tool (e.g., plopping open your Bible and searching the pages for an immediate answer to your crisis).

8. Judas believed the victories would testify that the Lord is the one who redeems and saves Israel.

9. The temple courts were desolate, the altar profaned, the gates burned, a thicket of bushes had grown up, and the chambers of the priests were in ruins.

10. Answers may vary. Anytime we experience success, we are liable to also experience pride, which may lead to a fall, as Scripture warns (Proverbs 16:18).

Day 3 • Read 1 Maccabees 6–9

11. In the first passage, the king bans the Judeans from following the practices of their faith and orders them to make themselves abominable. They even put to death those who continued to the old faith. In the second passage, the king describes himself as "kind and beloved in my power," although he also acknowledges that he had acted without good reason in punishing Judeans. He cannot see the extent of his sin, as none of us can (cf. Jeremiah 17:9).

12. Alcimus was stricken with paralysis and had to stop his demolition work. He could no longer speak, and he finally died.

13. (a & b) Answers will vary. This sort of plea for condemnation appears at times in Scripture and might be prayed. Yet Christ clearly teaches us in the New Testament to love and forgive our enemies and persecutors. When faced with challenges, we may not always easily discern which prayer accords with God's will.

14. (a) Judas contacted the Romans and sought an alliance with them. (b) Ultimately, the Romans came to Israel to rule, and they finally destroyed the temple.

15. (a) Jonathan succeeded his brother Judas. (b) The friends of Judas rallied to Jonathan and chose him as their new leader, which role Jonathan accepted.

Day 4 • Read 1 Maccabees 10–12

16. Seleucid King Alexander compels Jonathan to become high priest, which Jonathan welcomes. He becomes the leader in spiritual, political, and military realms. However, he was still subject to the Seleucid king.

17. (a) She is Cleopatra. (b) She is given as a wife to King Alexander in a political marriage intended to bring peace and good relations. She is, at this point, a political pawn. Cleopatra would eventually become the last pharaoh/Ptolemaic ruler of Egypt.

18. Jonathan used the disarray to seek control of Jerusalem. He gained help for battles from Seleucid troops. When he learned that Demetrius, the new Seleucid king, would depose him, Jonathan rebelled and experienced limited success.

19. The Spartans and Israelites assumed a "brotherhood" and even a family bond to each other, although there was no historic basis for this. They prayed for each other and each made offerings according to their different faiths.

20. Answers may vary. Paul warns against unholy alliances that would lead to mixing of religions.

Day 5 • Read 1 Maccabees 13–16

21. Israel became an independent kingdom for the first time since the conquest of Babylon in 587 BC.

22. There was peace, and Israel extended its borders to control its ancient territory. It was a time of prosperity.

23. The success is attributed to Simon rather than to the Lord.

24. Judas sought the counsel of God and pleaded for his help. Simon describes the success of his family in regaining the nation's independence and, as high priest, speaks a blessing, assuming God's help.

25. The Book of 1 Maccabees ends with political intrigue. Nehemiah ends with prayers to God about enemies of Israel, his commitment to God's ways, and a plea for God to do him good. One account is quite secular, the other depends on faith and God's favor.

The Lord Foiled Them by the Hand of a Woman

Judith

Preparing for the Session

Central Focus

Even the weakest person, armed with faith and strict adherence to the laws of Moses and the traditions of the elders, can defeat the most powerful Gentile enemies. Trust in God trumps armies of enemies.

Objectives

That participants, led by the Holy Spirit working through God's Word, will

1. remember that the One who dwells within them is stronger than the one who dwells in the world (1 John 4:4);
2. turn to the Lord for help and direction when faced with seemingly overwhelming problems; and
3. appreciate the resources given to them by God to do the work He gives them to do.

For the Small-Group Leader

Small-Group Discussion Helps

Day 1 • Read Judith 1:1–3:8

1. The writer describes the Assyrian army advancing as an unstoppable force.

2. The people dismissed him as though he was only one man and sent his messengers back to him without conceding anything.

3. Holofernes was a man of fear and terror who was fit to lead the king's unstoppable force.

4. They sent messengers requesting peace and vowing cooperation as Nebuchadnezzar's servants.

5. Holofernes was ordered to destroy all other gods so that people would worship only Nebuchadnezzar. Isaiah tells us that the Lord will not give His glory to another.

Day 2 • Read Judith 3:9–6:21

6. The Assyrian Empire was long gone by the time the Judeans returned from exile and rebuilt the temple (516 BC).

7. There is no reference to a king. Israel and Judah were monarchies during the era of the Assyrian empire. Instead, the high priest and Sanhedrin are acting together as the leaders of Israel, something that did not take place until after the exile and especially nearer the rise of the Maccabees.

8. They fasted, donned sackcloth, sprinkled themselves with ashes, repented of their sins, made offerings, and prayed for deliverance.

9. They had to fall into the same sin that would cause God to punish them.

10. Because the Assyrians didn't like Achior's counsel, they handed him over to the Israelites. They left him bound before the gates of Bethulia.

Day 3 • Read Judith 7–9

11. (a) They told Holofernes to capture and hold the water supply until the people of Bethulia wasted away. (b) This caused the Israelites to lose courage, turning their prayers into lamentations. They were ready to surrender.

12. Uzziah predicted that the Lord would be merciful to them within five days.

13. Judith was a widow who had lived without her husband, Manasseh, for about three years. During that time, she continued to mourn for her husband. She was both beautiful and well-off.

14. Answers may vary. The elders were provoking God to anger by taking an oath to surrender the city by a certain date. Judith trusted that the Lord would deliver them in His time.

15. (a & b) Answers may vary. Judith appealed to the examples of Simeon, who slew a village; requested consideration because she was a widow; and asked blessing on her deceit.

Day 4 • Read Judith 10:1–13:11

16. She would deceive Holofernes and his troops through charming them with beauty.

17. They were overwhelmed by her beauty and agreed to take her to Holofernes. They even began to admire the Israelites.

18. God would tell her when the Israelites had sinned and would be under God's wrath. She would then tell Holofernes so he could advance against them.

19. (a) Judith brought her own food and drink; she continued to observe the purity laws. (b) This was important because it made her credible as a pious Israelite who was in tune with Israel's God—part of her deceptive promise to Holofernes. It also was part of her faith to keep the Word so that He would not abandon her.

20. (a) Judith addresses God as almighty, "Lord God of Israel," and "God our God." (b) She had gotten away with the deception and execution of Holofernes she had planned.

Day 5 • Read Judith 13:11–16:25

21. Her beauty, sexual purity, hope, willingness to risk her life, vengeance of their ruin, and life walked in the straight path before God.

22. Achior identified the head as that of Holofernes, whom he had seen earlier.

23. Answers will vary. This could provoke a lively discussion. Measure the responses according to God's Word. If anything was fair, there would be no basis for protest of unfair treatment, massacres, atrocities against noncombatants. Chemical and biological weapons would be viewed as any other tools of war. Most participants will likely decide that not everything is fair in war.

24. The creation illustrates that God is almighty. It also reminds us that He made mankind male and female—an essential element of the story.

25. She refused to remarry but remained devoted to her departed husband. She was blessed with long life. She freed her maid (who was perhaps a house slave). She was generous to her family. Her accomplishment brought lasting safety to Israel.

Wisdom Is Radiant and Unfading

Wisdom of Solomon

Preparing for the Session

Central Focus

"The fear of the Lord is the beginning of wisdom" (Psalm 111:10). Acknowledging the one true God and submitting in faith to Him serves as the foundation for living in this world and being welcomed into eternal life when we die.

Objectives

That participants, led by the Holy Spirit working through God's Word, will

1. see the folly in placing anything above God in their lives;
2. find encouragement to "keep the faith" in the face of worldly pressure to abandon it; and
3. rejoice that Jesus Christ, the wisdom and power of God, has opened the way to eternal life through His death and resurrection.

For the Small-Group Leader

Small-Group Discussion Helps

Day 1 • Read Wisdom of Solomon 1:1–4:19

1. The Spirit of the Lord has filled the world with life, but God did not make death. The ungodly by their deeds and words summoned death.

2. Verses 6–20 include numerous examples in the "Let us" statements. They counsel a life of pleasure and exploitation of others. They also test God with their evil deeds.

3. The righteous will dwell at peace in God's presence, although God, who is merciful, will test them in this life. The ungodly will be punished. They will be miserable, hope in vain, and be unprofitable. Their families are cursed.

4. The Jews thought that righteousness was pleasing to God, who delivered Enoch from the threatening influence of evil. Enoch was "perfected." As with many things in the Apocrypha, these words may be correctly or incorrectly understood. Certainly, righteousness pleases God; but one must recognize it is also a gift of God and not a perfection we achieve by our own strength.

5. Wisdom is holy, honest, and kindly; it brings joy or contentment. The Lord watches out for the wise.

Day 2 • Read Wisdom of Solomon 4:20–8:21

6. Answers will vary. Allow participants to share their thoughts. Be careful not to let the discussion turn into uncharitable rants.

7. He wrote to chasten the rulers so that they would act wisely and not transgress God's Word.

8. Fix your thoughts on wisdom, seek her, act with vigilance, have concern for instruction, and keep her laws. Note that wisdom also is seeking to find you.

9. References to breath, emanation, and passing into holy souls all point to the Holy Spirit as wisdom in this passage.

10. *For personal reflection. Sharing optional.* Answers will vary. Allow sharing and discussion as time permits.

Day 3 • Read Wisdom of Solomon 9–12

11. Solomon is described in 1 Kings as asking God for wisdom rather than other benefits. The writer of Wisdom of Solomon describes himself as chosen by God to be king and to build a temple. He wishes to be worthy of the throne of his father. These circumstances fit Solomon.

12. (v. 1) Adam, (v. 3) Cain, (v. 4) Noah, (v. 5) Abraham, (v. 6) Lot, (v. 10) Jacob, and (v. 13) Joseph.

13. He used the animals they worshiped as the means for punishing them through the plagues.

14. God is a strong, great, merciful, loving creator. He is an immortal spirit present everywhere who reminds and warns so that people can be free from wickedness.

15. We should learn from the way God worked in the lives of the Old Testament saints, which shows He gives hope, punishes for the sake of repentance, gave covenant promises, and scourged enemies much more than His people.

Day 4 • Read Wisdom of Solomon 13:1–15:17

16. The unrighteous are foolish. They should know of God through His creation, which reveals His attributes (e.g., power, greatness, beauty). As a result, they are without excuse when they claim not to know Him.

17. God is also revealing His wrath against the unrighteous. God has given them up to their lusts because they preferred a lie to the truth. In contrast, Wisdom of Solomon says, "These people are little to be blamed" (13:6).

18. Answers may vary. Wit and humor are powerful tools, but they may also be self-defeating if they cause offense. Therefore, using them also requires wisdom and restraint.

19. Sin entered the world before wood or stone idols appeared. Yet one may argue that Adam and Eve made themselves idols when they sought to become like God. In this respect, idolatry is the beginning, means, and end of sin.

20. It means knowing that God will forgive you, that you will not want to sin. Knowing God is "complete righteousness . . . the root of immortality."

Day 5 • Read Wisdom of Solomon 15:18–19:22

21. He explains that the symbol was to remind them of God's Law. The sight of the symbol was not what saved. Instead, the Lord who commanded its creation saved them (16:6–7).

22. It punishes the unrighteous but relaxes for the faithful. Through the Word, the Lord feeds us (cf. Jesus' statement in Matthew 4:4).

23. Fear is surrender of the help that comes from reason.

24. They valued the sacrifices, confessed their faith in God's Word ("divine law"), shared with one another in abundance and poverty, and shared stories of their forbearers' examples, which were worthy of praise.

25. It was like a new creation, complying with God's command. He played the elements of the creation as one plays a harp, changing the elements in one respect (as a musician may change a rhythm) but keeping the elements the same otherwise (since changing rhythm does not change the notes; B flat remains B flat whether one plays the rhythm of a march, jazz, rock, or a samba).